Daniel Jenkins

Christian Maturity
and the
Theology of Success

SCM PRESS LTD

334 00152 8

First published 1976
by SCM Press Ltd
56 Bloomsbury Street London WC1

© SCM Press 1976

Filmset in 'Monophoto' Ehrhardt 10 on 11 pt by
Richard Clay (The Chaucer Press) Ltd, Bungay, Suffolk
and printed in Great Britain by
Fletcher & Son Ltd, Norwich

Christian Maturity and the Theology of Success

Contents

This book is a revised version of the Warfield Lectures given at Princeton Theological Seminary from 31 March to 4 April 1975. I should like to express my gratitude to the members of the Seminary community for their hospitality and their extremely kind reception, especially to my old friends Dr James I. McCord, Dr James Hastings Nichols and Dr Erik Routley. The help I received from those members of Regent Square United Reform Church and the 1662 Society in London, who sat through a repetition of the Lectures on six hot Sunday evenings in the remarkable summer of 1975, should also be acknowledged. My daughter Caroline did a great deal of typing and made many useful comments.

D.J.

I

Faith and Success

Few people think readily in these days of any connection between Christian faith and what is commonly thought of as success. In European lands, churches have suffered from prolonged institutional decline, with the result that their leaders have not claimed much public attention and their theologians have become self-critical. Even in America, where the institutional situation is very different, professional theologians recoil in horror from anything which hints at the power of positive thinking. The dangers of ecclesiastical triumphalism, the attitude which does not make a sharp enough distinction between the kingdom of God and the earthly church, have been a staple theme of the ecumenical movement for over a generation. Nowadays, Roman Catholic theologians vie with those of the Reformed tradition in emphasizing that theirs is a theology of the cross rather than one of glory. Churchmen in Africa and Asia and South America have been at pains to assert their solidarity with the poor, the dispossessed and those struggling to obtain political power, and their influence has been dominant in the World Council of Churches in recent years. People outside the Christian community often think of the church as an institution on the defensive, whose representatives lack the self-confidence which comes from familiarity with the sweet smell of success.

This situation has regrettable consequences. Christians themselves come to think of maturity not as a present possession, a gift from their Lord, but as the object of vague aspiration, something seen only by contrast with the immaturity which is our normal state. This means that they give little attention to what follows after they have discovered and obeyed what they believe to be the will of God. This book will try to show that this both hinders them from making the most of resources they already possess and from facing the distinctive

1

temptations to which they are exposed, those which arise from the successful fulfilment of their vocation.

A few recent theologians have hinted at a different approach, but they have done no more than that. Bonhoeffer has a short passage in his *Ethics* entitled 'The Successful Man'[1] but, despite the extremely affirmative view of life and its possibilities under God which he was increasingly taking at that time, it deals mainly with the contrast between the crucified Christ and the world's understanding of success. Heinrich Ott, basing himself on Bonhoeffer, picks up the theme in his *Reality and Faith*[2] only to discard it without further discussion. Karl Barth, the outstanding systematic theologian of the last generation, is pre-eminently the theologian who sees Christian maturity in terms of success. His theology is rightly described by G. C. Berkouwer as that of 'the triumph of grace'.[3] We shall be drawing extensively in this discussion on those great quarries, still inadequately mined, of the third and fourth volumes of his major work, the *Church Dogmatics* for a great deal of our material but even he does not deal with the matter directly and ignores many of its aspects.[4]

The New Testament is, above all else, a success story. This is why the gospels are given their name. They are good tidings of great joy. Yet it is a success very different from any which the world knows. It is won only through the most radical kind of apparent failure against the strongest of opponents and it also confronts those who participate in this success with a whole new range of difficulties, which only become visible as a result of that success. The gospels make little sense until it is seen that they are addressed primarily to believers, those who already share in a measure of the success of Christ, those who are, therefore, the rich, the heirs of the kingdom, who have begun to enjoy the glorious liberty of the children of God. It is only when this is grasped that the full originality of their warnings against the perils of riches can be appreciated. The natural human temptation is to misunderstand these by assuming that they must refer primarily to others rather than to ourselves, those who happen to be materially better off than we are or who have some position or privilege which we covet for ourselves or, more insidiously, for someone else whom we consider more deserving than their present possessors. But in this context such distinctions are trivial. Whatever his worldly circumstances may be, anyone who has the spirit of Christ and who is an heir of the eternal covenant is rich.[5] Our riches may be more spiritual than material and may themselves be the fruit of the purest faith, yet they remain riches, and the awful warning 'how hardly shall they that have riches enter the kingdom of God' still speaks to our condition. This is true even though we are already the beneficiaries of the kingdom, in the way the rich young ruler himself was. The mature Christian is precisely the one who knows that he is rich and who enjoys his riches and becomes richer in the process and who also knows that this makes his position before God all the more precarious, so that he is driven back constantly to the realization that all this is possible only through God's grace, made clear in the cross and resurrection of Jesus Christ.

This central truth in the teaching of Jesus concerning the kingdom is exemplified in the experience of the apostle Paul, whose letters are particularly revealing in this respect. Again, it is essential to realize that Paul is the rich man, the Hebrew of the Hebrews who is aware of being an heir of the promises made to Abraham. The self-consciousness which leads to an awareness of radical contradiction and which prompted him to develop the great argument of the first eight chapters of Romans, was the product not of weakness, of a slave mentality, but of the seriousness which comes from strength. It was Nietzsche's failure to see this which led him so completely to misunderstand Paul, whom he regarded as an outstanding example of the resentment which arises from spiritual failure. Paul has the conscience of the rich and he is trying to face the difficulties which arise because of the burden of riches. As with Job before him, these arise precisely because of his faithfulness to his vocation and he is vindicated only because he refuses to allow them to make him forsake his vocation. The more seriously he tries to follow the God-given law, the deeper becomes his sense of responsibility and his moral insight, and the more aware he becomes of falling short. Grace comes to him as release from the existential tension caused by this apparently insoluble moral dilemma, but he would not have known this grace unless he had had the strength to face this dilemma without flinching. When it does come in these circumstances, it is immensely creative, as the eighth chapter of Romans makes so vividly clear. Yet, as the Corinthian church drives him almost to despair by failing to see, it remains creative only if it continues to be seen as grace, making us aware of the new dangers which arise in consequence of the very victories which have been won for us. Maturity has really been given to mankind. This is set forth in the widest possible setting in the daring claims made by the letter to the Ephesians. We have been set free and, as the letter to the Galatians insists, must never be

3

content to settle for less than the full freedom which maturity demands. But that freedom is not now a natural possession. Because it is known only in Christ, it can only find expression in constant struggle with all those forces which deny Christ, both within ourselves and in our dealings with each other and the world around us. As with all the workings of grace, we genuinely possess this maturity, yet do so only as we overcome evidences of immaturity or misuses of new-found power which arise as we move further along the road to its full realization.

This is one reason why we need the guidance of the Spirit. The Pauline writings are also notable for their emphasis on how necessary and many-sided the resources of the Spirit are if we are to attain to mature humanity, 'to the measure of the stature of the fulness of Christ'.[6] The way in which the Spirit works makes clear two aspects of the nature of Christian maturity which are vital to the development of this whole argument. The first is that this maturity is known only in relationship. Our humanity is co-humanity. As I Corinthians 12 and Ephesians 4 emphasize, the gifts of the Spirit are given to each only for the sake of all, because it is together and not separately that those who follow Christ achieve mature manhood. In this, the Pauline writings are reflecting the teaching of the Bible as a whole. This unity in community is implied in the teaching of Jesus concerning the kingdom and, as Barth has so extensively argued,[7] it is in this sense that Christians are to understand the second creation story in Genesis.

Secondly, because maturity is discovered only in relationship, we have a mutual interest in each other's growth towards maturity. Spiritual gifts are provided for the building up of the body of Christ, his instrument for expressing the service of God in the world. Without this building up, we remain undeveloped, 'children, tossed by the waves and whirled about by every fresh gust of teaching, dupes of crafty rogues and their deceitful schemes'.[8] As we shall see more fully when we come to consider the church as a school of maturity, the Christian community is meant to be the place where, above all others, fellow-members of Christ neither keep each other down nor do each other down but build each other up, as the necessary condition of growth toward a common maturity.

Because it possesses this communal character, the liberation which Christian maturity brings has always to be expressed in specific terms. We are not released into an abstract freedom, like prisoners who suddenly find themselves outside the prison gate one cold morn-

4

ing with nothing to do and nowhere to go and no one to meet them. Nor are we left simply to celebrate and stay with and constantly try to re-live the experience of liberation itself. This is what romanticism supposes, whether in religious or secular guise, a supposition which is having one of its frequent revivals in our own time. As Barth emphasizes in his great discussion of freedom in *Church Dogmatics* IV.3, one is released only to discover one's vocation and it is always a vocation which has reference to the community. The recovery of freedom means the recovery of the power of choice and choice, once made, inevitably carries with it limitation. One goes here and not there, does this and not that. The calling is for a particular purpose and any gifts which are received are intended to help with the fulfillment of that purpose. What is more, not only does choice involve limitation but limitations are imposed on the range of options open to one because of the nature of one's calling. Freedom is freedom for one's neighbour, the release from self-preoccupation to be available for one's neighbour, to become a 'man for others'. It is the neighbour's needs, and the positive possibilities of constructive action which open up in association with the neighbour, which condition the nature of the choice. 'Permissiveness', as it is called today, or 'licence' as it used to be called, is the irresponsibly selfish attempt to break out from the pattern of mutual obligation in which freedom alone has any meaning, using as its excuse the fact that, as always happens in life, some older patterns of meaning have become unnecessarily restrictive and need to be looked at afresh. In Pauline terms, such an attitude is not one of freedom but of enslavement, and enslavement not to the law but to what he means by the flesh, arbitrarily self-centred existence. Even when the individual's vocation may demand a creative break-through into the unknown which has to be taken alone and when it may seem to go against the will of most of his fellows, as such break-throughs often do, it will still have reference to the community. Only God can call anyone to such a vocation and the Lord's Prayer explicitly warns us to pray that we may be spared such a test. To take it upon oneself, casting off the support of the community, is to tempt God. Part of the meaning of the cross is that Jesus has now gone before us to endure that particular trial alone. Those who demand in their pride, like Thomas, to see his hands and his side before being prepared to receive his peace and his commission and his Spirit, show that they are not to be trusted with that isolation.

The more fully it works out in practice, the more the liberation of the Christian expresses itself in identification with one's neighbour and in the overcoming of alienation both from him and from the place in which one has been placed in life as a result of one's vocation. The notion of alienation has usually been discussed with reference to the Marxist analysis of the relation between the workman and his skill or, more recently, to what constitutes mental health, but in Christian terms, it refers primarily to our relation with God and, through him, with each other and with the natural order. What happens must not be over-simplified. On the one hand, anyone who has heard the call of Christ is made more acutely aware of alienation than he was before. As he comes to himself, it becomes clear to him how far he has strayed from his home, and how long the road back has to be. But he sees this only when he knows that the way back is now open, that his past failures have been forgiven and that his father is ready to restore him. The last thing he will be tempted to do, therefore, is to take pride in being alienated and to tell stories of how excitingly tough life was among the swine when they shared their husks with him and to contrast it with the unadventurous dullness of the life of his stay-at-home elder brother.

The notion of identification has also been much discussed recently, often in the same context, but sometimes in as distorted a way as that of alienation. Everything depends on whom one identifies with and the way in which one does it. The mature Christian will realize that it is possible even to use an act of identification as a way of expressing covert alienation, a demonstration against someone who will disapprove of one's action rather than a genuine commitment to the one with whom one appears to be identifying oneself. This is why the rule has to be that true identification begins with one's nearest neighbours, those for whom one has the most direct responsibility, and those, therefore, in relation to whom one is likely to feel most alienated, especially if they belong to a different age-group, race, church, social class or level of education from oneself.[9] It is with these that reconciliation is likely to be most difficult, most undramatic, and ultimately most rewarding. As Jesus said to the Syro-Phoenician woman in his semi-ironical conversation with her, his first vocation was to the house of Israel, with the implication that it is only when one has managed to straighten out relations with those who are nearest that one has a basis from which to begin to have a genuinely helpful relation to those who are further away, although, as she reminded him in one of the few incidents in scripture where Jesus is successfully answered in kind, they also may have a claim on one's attention.[10] What this might mean for relations between Christians and Jews is still an unresolved, and inexcusably neglected, issue. What it means for social and political priorities has to be determined by each Christian individual and group in its own situation.[11]

The communal nature of Christian liberation, and the fact that we need all the gifts of the Spirit granted to the community if we are not again to be led astray, also throws light on the relation between the strength which seems to come directly from Christ in the Spirit and what appears to be ordinary human strength. By the latter is meant the capacity to handle oneself and one's relation with one's neighbour and with the world around oneself in ways which compel the respect of the Christian believer when he looks out on the world from his own point of view. There is obviously a great deal of strength in the world which does not seem to stem directly from Christian inspiration. What its origins are, and what its relation is to the exclusive Christian claim to salvation, are important questions which cannot here concern us. The two points to be made which are relevant to this argument are these. The first is that, in so far as this is genuine strength and not a proud attempt at self-sufficiency or dominance, the mature Christian is glad to find it and welcome it as an added resource to what he already knows through the Spirit. As Bonhoeffer came to see so clearly, nothing is more base than for the Christian to suppose that the honour of his faith demands that he disparage such strength and seek to undermine it because it did not originate within his own community. The success of the disciples of the crucified Christ may be very different from success as the world normally understands it, but there are some forms of success to be found in the world which survive the crucified Christ's test and, when they do, we can be sure that they receive his blessing. Fortunately for us, God has dealings with his children independently of professional Christians.[12] By the same token, however, the other point also holds. Such strength is at least as vulnerable as any more directly generated within the Christian community. The so-called 'secular' rich man will not find it any easier to enter the kingdom than the religious rich man. Our faith should train us to detect the kind of strength we find in Christ wherever it appears in the world, and then so identify ourselves with those who possess it that we can share with them, in the ways most acceptable to them, the resources we possess from Christ to help make the most of that strength and overcome the difficulties which it creates.

The fact that Christ came not to call the righteous but sinners to repentance does not contradict the truth of this. His words were addressed ironically to those whom the world calls righteous, those who are strong as mankind knows strength, and the implication is that their very strength should make them see his point. They, above all people, should be able to understand why he set about his mission in the way he did, since their very strength should make them realize their vulnerability and their need for grace. It is they who see most clearly that the kingdom can only be entered by those who have become as little children. For example, there is an element of humbug in protestations of humility on the part of those who are weak. As the saying is, they so obviously have so many things to be humble about that there is no need for them to call attention to the fact. When they do so, it is hard to avoid the suspicion that they are doing so either out of self-pity or in order to gain a hidden advantage over the strong by making them feel guilty. The qualities displayed by maturity in weakness are not so much those of humility as those of patience, courage and independence of spirit. It is very hard for a human being to be honestly humble and it is most likely to arise when, in freedom, we fulfil our vocation to the limit of our capacity and have to confess that, having done all, we remain unprofitable servants.[13] This is why it is generally those who achieve most, especially in the arts and sciences, who are often the most unaffectedly humble, because the more they penetrate into the mystery of existence, the more they realize how much there is still to discover and how much they depend on insights which come from beyond themselves if they are to find any of it.

It was because his task was so great that Jesus was able to see it so unreservedly in terms of service and this is why his example of humility carries so much conviction. It was because he did not consider it a prize to be greedily snatched at to be on an equality with God,[14] because, as we might say, he was so sure of his status and had such a tremendous work to do, that he was free to take the form of a bond-slave and there to suffer humiliation and death. Those who possess the power, the *exousia*, of Christ should be able to do the same.

Apart from anything else, it is only when they start from this position of assured strength that they can presume to undertake the hazardous, and possibly invidious, role of being the servants of their fellows. We are told to fear the Greeks when they come bearing gifts but the same is true of all gift-bearers, and Christians are no exceptions. Indeed, the greater the gift, the greater the danger, for giver and receiver. Even if his service is itself free from servility, it can easily encourage it in those at the receiving end if the terms of the gift are not properly made clear. However genuinely the Christian may set out only to serve, the service itself can quickly become a justifying work which leads him to develop a vested interest in having a suitable number of servees in a dependent relation. The fact that this happens with groups no less than with individuals, as the history of many service agencies in society makes all too clear, only complicates the matter further. This is why it is so important that Christians should see both that the impulse to serve should arise from strength and that its concern should be the restoration or the evocation of strength. The service is successful only when it is rendered without losing the respect of the one served and when his self-respect and power of independent action are built up in the process.[15]

The classical Reformed teaching about justification by faith is particularly helpful at this very point because it insists that the root of the impulse to serve others lies, not in the desire to justify ourselves, but in gratitude to God for the way in which we ourselves have been helped. That gratitude in its turn is made sincere and humble because it knows that we were helped in a situation where we were quite unable to help ourselves. The parable which is commonly taken as the most clear directive to Christian service is that of the Good Samaritan, but it teaches a falsely patronizing idea of service if we identify ourselves, as most of us are disposed to do, too readily with the Samaritan, usually forgetting his disreputable 'outsider' status as we do so. Jesus asked the lawyer who put the original self-justifying question to place himself in the situation of the man who fell among thieves, where he was grateful for any help given without questions asked and where he could do nothing in return. We shall miss the force of the parable unless we try to do the same. It is grace apprehended on this level which alone produces authentic Christian service and it is only as we strive to continue to conform all our activities to this grace, even after our service has evoked gratitude in its turn, that we can express the liberation which is in Christ and grow towards mature humanity.

9

2

The Qualities of Maturity

The New Testament, as we have said, is a success story. Even the Passion narrative, Karl Barth has argued, is misread unless it is placed firmly within the setting of a celebration of the royal majesty of Christ.[1] It makes clear the nature of the new life which is open to mankind through Jesus Christ, as the realization of mature humanity, while at the same time revealing the radical terms on which alone it can be enjoyed. This is the central theme of the whole New Testament but it is stated most directly in terms of the particular interest of this book in the Sermon on the Mount and in some of the brief ethical exhortations to be found in Paul's letters. It is on these that our exposition will chiefly rely.

In considering first some passages from the Sermon on the Mount, we must remind ourselves again that it is addressed to members of the new Israel, who abound in the riches and strength of the heirs of an eternal covenant. This may not be immediately obvious because the Sermon opens with references to the blessedness of those who are poor in spirit and who suffer poverty and persecution in this life. These are solemn warnings that Christian success is very different from success according to the world's reckoning and that it always carries with it a share in the burden Christ bore. In their own place, these warnings will always demand the most serious attention of all Christians. What is significant for our present purpose, however, is the speed with which the mood changes to a more positive, it might almost be called a more light-hearted, one, which remains dominant throughout the rest of the Sermon. Unless this is seen it is hard to make sense of some of the most familiar passages, yet they make complete sense when it is. The result of failure to see this has been a great deal of anxiety, and misplaced heroics, on the part of many Christians who take with unimaginative literalness as austere moral demands passages which are meant to be liberating and joyful.

This can be illustrated first by reference to one of the Beatitudes themselves: 'Blessed are the meek, for they shall inherit the earth.' Meekness is taken today to be a quality of the weak. The meek are the passive, the spineless, those born to be put upon, nature's doormats. How could the likes of them inherit the earth, and why indeed should they? Their inclination is always to retreat from power and they would not know what to do with the earth if they did inherit it. The most they could do would be to discover some perverse strength fired by resentment, the worm turning, rarely an effective, and never an attractive quality, well worthy of the contempt poured on it by Nietzsche. But this, of course is not what the passage means at all, any more than it is what similar passages in the Magnificat mean. 'Meekness' in the seventeenth century was a quality of strength and the word used is now better translated, as the New English Bible does, 'those of gentle spirit'. An appropriate picture to have in interpreting this Beatitude is that of the gentle giant, a large heavy athlete, who wants to win the confidence and inspire the affection and obtain the co-operation of a timid little girl. He lowers his voice and carefully controls his cumbersome movements, perhaps even getting down on his knees, so that he can allay her fears and make it easy for her to communicate with him. When he can make her see that his strength is under the control of his gentle will and that all he wants to do is to help her and enjoy her company, then the strength becomes a reassurance rather than a threat. She becomes the stronger because of it and a constructive relationship is now possible.

It is very significant for understanding what Christian obedience means in terms of politics and public affairs at the present time that this Beatitude should be placed in immediate conjunction with one which praises those who hunger and thirst after righteousness, or that the right should prevail. Those who are themselves liberated rightly desire to help others find liberation, initially that fundamental liberation which Christ brings but one which also has repercussions for liberation from oppression on all the levels of ordinary life in the world. This will give them a passion that the right will prevail, a passion which is likely to intensify as they find that their new life endows them with the insight and courage and perseverence which bring success. This passion, it is important to note, Jesus calls a blessing to those who possess it and it will bring results. The right will prevail. Yet, like other blessings, it has its dangers. Nothing is easier than to overwhelm even those we wish to help with our own zeal. In the process, they may be forced to conform to our interpretation of what their liberation should mean and lose sight of their own vocation, as those who are answerable to God in their own right. In the end, if no limit is set to our passion, all that will happen is that they exchange one servitude for another, with the added tribulation that they are expected to show gratitude to their new conquerors for delivering them from their former masters.

This is why it matters that those who have a zeal for righteousness should also be those of gentle spirit. This is true in directly personal relationships and no less true in political, and especially international, affairs. Only those who have transcended themselves sufficiently to have a gentle spirit can be trusted to have their hunger and thirst that the right should prevail satisfied because they realize that the right is not simply their own possession and that liberation for others means having room for discovering their own vocation without interference even by their liberators. It is also being brought home to us with increasing force today that this has application not only to human relations but also to the relation of humanity as a whole to the natural order. If mankind refuses to deal with nature in a gentle spirit but arrogantly rips out her secrets and plunders her to satisfy its every unconsidered whim, on the assumption that this is automatically righteous, its dominion over nature will be taken away and it will find that it no longer inherits the earth.

The other Beatitude which singles out a particularly significant quality of Christian maturity is that which says, 'Blessed are the peacemakers, for they shall be called the children of God', for the making of peace is integral to growth into full maturity. Peace, in Augustine's phrase, is the tranquillity of order but the Bible would not understand this in the static, hierarchical sense it has sometimes held in the course of Christian history. It is that unity of heart and mind which enables us to work and grow together, the peace of an ideal family which the Spirit-sustained church is meant to enjoy, conveyed by the great biblical word, *shalom*. The New Testament sees the world left to itself as always in process of slipping back into that primeval chaos, that radical disorder, where there is no meaning and no significant purpose, out of which it was originally called by God. When people are at odds with each other, they are caught up in that process. In such situations, the limitation, or preferably the halting, of their hostilities, may initially be the only thing to be done, but no one should be under any illusion that that in itself constitutes the making of peace. As Jacques Ellul has reminded us in his study of violence,[2] the letting loose of brute force to have its own way is not patient of Christian resolution. Peace becomes a possibility only when the violence stops and people are able to treat each other as human beings again, to listen to each other, to adjust their attitudes to each other and to build up sufficient confidence in each other to make and hope to keep agreements. This is why, as again Ellul points out, a great deal of Christian peace-making has to be quiet and unspectacular. Even trying to mediate between conflicting groups and individuals, which Christians will often be led to do, is only a second-best, an attempt to make up for earlier failures in true peace-making. A mature understanding of what making peace involves will lead Christians to be far-sighted, sensitive and vigilant, always looking well ahead and having efficient early warning systems about where breakdowns in relationship might occur and violent conflict ensue and ready to move in quickly before all communication breaks down. Violent conflict is sometimes inevitable but when it occurs it is an occasion for penitence for all concerned. When it is brought to an end, the result cannot in itself be a victory in any sense which a Christian can recognize, however much he may welcome it if he supports what appears to be the winning side. It is no more than the end of a damaging emergency, like the putting out of a fire. The possibility of a victory for righteousness only arises when the terms of the new relationship which emerges from the conflict are considered. Does it make for the building of peace?

All this should be obvious enough in a Christian context but it is disturbing that it should be lost sight of in some of the romanticization of violence which takes place in Christian circles today, often curiously claiming that this is a particularly radical form of Christianity in doing so. It is true that in one very radical sense Jesus brought not peace but a sword, but it was the sword of God's word, dividing between the joints and the marrow of the intents of the heart. It was no club with which to batter the outsides of people into physical submission. The Christian life is a matter of conflict with evil and issues have to be faced and sometimes they have to be forced. Christians themselves may disagree and have to go their separate ways. That happened, we are told, even with Paul and Barnabas, and Barnabas was 'a good man, full of the Holy Ghost and of faith'. Nor can Christians stand aside when the clash of conflicting powers is involved, even when the power involves the use of violence. Situations may arise when they have to become 'freedom fighters', or when they may think it right to support 'freedom fighters'. Yet all the time, they will not lose sight of the fact that, however close the relation may be between the two in some contexts, that freedom is never the same as the freedom already given in Christ, a freedom which gives them a distinctive expertise in making peace rather than war. The Christian's radicalism does not prompt him to go out into the world with a chip on his shoulder, spoiling for a fight, but enables him to look for the root of the difficulty in a troubled situation to see whether it can be removed. Knowing the importance of self-criticism, especially when one is consumed by a zeal for righteousness, he should be able to see possibilities of communication and fresh understanding in situations of conflict and have patience to work for their realization. He will know how intractable human nature is, especially in its self-justifying moods, and he will expect the work of making peace to be slow and difficult and he will allow for setbacks without discouragement. He will also know that when peace in a particular situation is achieved, it will remain precarious. He will not be surprised when a new threat emerges, because there is no abiding peace on earth. Yet he will persevere, because the making of peace, which reflects the enduring divine order in the midst of the broken fragments of human orders, remains the most rewarding of all human activities.

When peace-making is looked at in this way, a totally different set of priorities from that which prevails among the most politically 'militant' groups in society will then become established among Christians. More attention will be paid to strengthening positions of health and stability and to avoiding the complacency which erodes that health and stability than to those situations of crisis and break-down which inevitably capture the headlines and invite spectacular action. In a world where many people are only too ready to blow up their neighbours, and sometimes themselves, in order to prove that their cause is alone the righteous one, they will have the maturity to cultivate the arts of diplomacy, of thoughtfulness, coolness and unwearying patience, and give their strongest moral support to those who, whether they bear a Christian name or not, display those qualities in human affairs. These are the keepers of peace, who make possible the activities of the makers of peace.

The third quality of maturity is generosity. Some of the most familiar passages in the Sermon on the Mount provide examples of how this quality is to be exercised. I refer particularly to turning the other cheek, giving one's shirt as well as one's coat and walking the second mile, and also to the warnings against anxiety about food and drink and clothing. The whole spirit of these passages is lost if they are taken as calls to heroic self-sacrifice. They are put forward cheerfully, one might almost say in an off-hand way, as though Jesus is not expecting his followers to find what he is saying either surprising or difficult to put into practice. These are words spoken to the rich, who are being told to behave with the confident style and open-handed generosity appropriate to their status and their great expectations. When they are told to turn the other cheek, it is misleading to have a picture of someone suffering a rain of blows with drawn face and an air of martyrdom. It is true that the Christian who follows his Lord will sometimes be called to suffer in exactly that way, taking into himself all the weight of the evil in a particular situation, so that it dies there and is carried no further. The last of the Beatitudes emphasizes and reiterates this[3] and, coming immediately after the Beatitude on peace-making, suggests that the peace-maker may well find that such persecution will often be part of his lot. But this is surely not where the emphasis lies in these particular passages. For example, in turning the other cheek, I think again of the gentle giant, perhaps a big, good-humoured, craggy boxer, against whom a small boy is testing his strength. When the boy hits him as hard as he can on one side of the face, he laughs and turns the other cheek, saying, 'Come on, hit harder. See if you can hurt me this time.' Jesus is reminding his hearers that, with the resources of their strength, they can afford to be generous.

Similarly, the warnings about anxiety at the end of the sixth chapter of Matthew are not a call either to heroic austerity or to that kind of anxiety which is sometimes called 'living by faith', where people serving a good cause spend so much time praying for the cheque mysteriously to drop through the letter-box at the last minute that their very prayer becomes a form of worry. What Jesus is saying is that worry is the congenital vice of the rich and that it is basely and stupidly unnecessary. What have they got to worry about? They have plenty. If even the lilies of the field are taken care of, surely the heirs of the kingdom can take their economic problems in their stride and not have to spend time and energy in bothering about them. They literally have better things to think about. To seek God's kingdom and his righteousness will produce the creative unrest which generates sufficient energy to allow them to organize their temporal affairs without difficulty. They will have that detachment in relation to everyday things and that assurance concerning God's goodness which will give them the margin which enables them to be generous.

In their freedom from worry, the heirs of the kingdom have the will as well as the means to be generous. Here what has already been said about gratitude as the impulse to service becomes important. Gratitude makes one want to share what one has received with others, not merely because it is right but because one needs the others to join in the celebration and add to the delight. Gratitude overflowing in delight is irresistible. When the Christian comes bearing gifts in this spirit, there is no need to fear him because all hint of patronage is removed and equality is confirmed. All are enriched and all grow in stature. Nothing is further from the spirit of the Sermon on the Mount than the censorious meanness of the rich who, having put their trust in riches, become obsessed with anxiety about their safety, doling out even their charity with strings carefully attached and sensing potential subversion behind every begging bowl. This is not to say that giving can be thoughtless. In our last section we shall have to consider why to give well has to be treated as an art, which needs more cultivation than it normally receives. What is essential is that the spirit in which one gives should express the life-enhancing generosity appropriate to the way in which one has received.

For the fourth quality of maturity we turn to the letter to the Philippians where, warning his readers against anxiety in the same way as the Sermon on the Mount does, Paul says in a concluding exhortation, 'Let your *epieikēs* be manifest to all'.[4] The elusiveness of this quality of *epieikēs* is indicated by the difficulties which the translators have had with it. It has been variously rendered 'moderation', 'tolerance', 'forbearance' and as in the New English Bible and perhaps best of all, 'magnanimity'.[5] Each of these lights up a different aspect, but magnanimity may be best because it brings out the element of largeness of spirit, reflecting the divine fullness and, as we have seen, expressing itself in generosity, which is central to the notion of maturity. The context is significant. 'Rejoice in the Lord always, again I say, rejoice. Let your magnanimity be manifest to all. The Lord is near. Have no anxiety but in everything make your requests known to God in prayer and petition with thanksgiving. And the peace of God which passes understanding will keep guard over your heart and your thoughts in Christ Jesus.' It is important not to miss the eschatological reference. He is saying: 'You know Christ's victorious power and rejoice in it. He is at hand. The final resolution of all things is imminent. In all this, you possess already that peace, that inward harmony, which nothing in the world can destroy because it comes from God and is protected by Christ himself. This is why you can show magnanimity. You recognize that all your actions and judgments have to be provisional. You could be wrong and your neighbour could be wrong but you need not worry unduly about this. The Lord, with whom you are in contact and who knows your situation, will set it right when he comes and his will is one of grace and forgiveness. Even if your neighbour *is* wrong, therefore, and especially if he has offended you, you do not need to be too officious in setting him right. Since he is so near at hand, you are free to anticipate the Lord's forgiveness. And anyway, you know that nothing that any wrongdoer does can violate the peace in your heart and your thoughts over which Christ stands guard. In your strength, you can afford to be magnanimous, tolerant, forbearing, free from a fanatical zeal for righteousness, moderate'.

It hardly needs to be underlined how important this quality is in a time when passions are aroused and people are filled with a zeal for righteousness which lacks gentleness of spirit and generosity, making them more concerned that their own conception of what is right should prevail than that it should make for peace. It provides a justification for Christian support of what are sometimes called 'moderate' or 'liberal' policies, particularly in the political sphere where matters which are essentially relative can easily be absolutized. To say this, however, is not to offer a euphemism for mere mediocrity, which never knows when to make a stand or to sharpen an issue when the situation demands it. Reinhold Niebuhr demonstrated in ways which have been forgotten with depressing rapidity in some sections of the Christian community that 'moderate' and 'liberal' policies in the kind of social democracy in which such policies must readily prevail are a mark not of timidity and the refusal to face the responsibilities of power but of a high maturity and a realistic appraisal both of the potentialities and the dangers of political action.[6] This maturity is magnanimous and forbearing as well as moderate, concerned to look beyond a particular conflict to seek a basis on which peace can be built, because its eschatological perspective enables it to see further than the eyes of those who are concerned only with what they conceive to be justice now, and on their own terms. It is not swayed by the adolescent temptation to absolutize its own insights and then to lose patience and seek an outlet for its frustrations in violence when things do not work out exactly as it expected. It is this magnanimity, much more than the power of government so much emphasized by traditionalist theologians as a dyke against sin, which helps to preserve the world unto the day of judgment and it does so, as the apostle implies, through anticipating the nature of that merciful judgment by the way in which it handles power here and now.

The fact that it arises in the context of eschatological expectation is what makes this quality of *epieikēs* so different from the luke-warmness and mediocrity with which it might easily be confused. What that expectation does is not to encourage the deferment of decision but to intensify experience.[7] Knowing that the Lord is near means that judgment is also near. The good and the evil are seen to be ripening together unto the day of judgment and, as the gospels constantly insist, this gives urgency to decisions here and now. The goodness of the good and the evil of the evil stand out all the more clearly and the time is short in which to make clear where one stands. Yet all this takes place with the knowledge that the judgment is not ours but the Lord's and that we shall be judged along with our opponents, and judged after the manner of Christ's dealings when he was in the midst of mankind. This makes us vigilant and alert, delivering us from quietism as well as from fanaticism, making our action in the affairs of this life incisive and to the point and, because it is informed by charity, essentially constructive. As Karl Barth has shown so superbly in his long discussion of 'Man in his Time',[8] it gives us the ability to do the right thing at the right time and also the composure to be content to wait when waiting is the only thing left to do.

Because it is so forward-looking, it also enables us to be delivered from any temptation to seek revenge. We need not nurse resentment when we suffer a defeat, resentment which diminishes our own stature and undermines all hope of making peace, and we can afford to be magnanimous in victory. Liberation is prize enough and one wants to share it even with those who previously stood in the way of its achievement. In the light of the knowledge that the Lord is near, it is silly to behave like the new rich who take pleasure in looking down on those who previously looked down on them. We have the promise, and the warning, that when the Lord comes such behaviour will quickly meet its deserts.[9]

The eschatological perspective also gives the necessary detachment, the sense of holding oneself in, the forbearance, which is also an element of *epieikēs*, and which prevents us from being the prisoners of our own time. Such imprisonment means, as the New Testament would say, subjection to the powers of this present age. It safeguards the more impressionable amongst us against mere trendiness, which may give the illusion of progressive movement but which is, in fact, no more than being swayed from side to side, being 'tossed to and fro by every gust of teaching', the opposite of growth towards maturity. Instead of panting after the spirit of the age, we press towards our own goal and this enables us to foresee things which are to come, after the manner of the prophets, and to be prepared to meet them.

Finally, maturity is joyful. 'Rejoice in the Lord always, and again I say, rejoice.' This is a theme which resounds through the whole New Testament, standing in the strongest contrast to the joylessness of much life today, vacillating as it does between the moody discontent of adolescence and the self-pitying cynicism of unhappy old age, a joylessness sometimes reflected in the internal life of the Christian community. It is a joy of anticipation of the glory to come, which is so great that it overflows into a zest for life here and now. It cannot wait until the new life 'to be clothed upon with its habitation which is from above' and starts trying to live now as though it were already there, transforming its temporary resting places on this earth into the image of the homeland. The significance of this for the Christian attitude to play and to celebration of the Lord's day will be considered in the last section. As Paul himself understood so well, this joy is always experienced in the midst of trouble,[10] yet when he is not having directly to put up with trouble,[11] the mature Christian should be filled with the strength which comes from joy, setting forth every morning, like the sun in the psalms, as a strong man to run a race.

More than that, as Paul goes on to remind his readers in the very next verses of the passage in Philippians which we have been discussing, this positive, confident attitude enables us to appreciate and make the most of all that we find good in the life of the world and the human heritage. We are to reflect on 'whatsoever is true and noble and just and pure and loveable and gracious and excellent and admirable'. In this one sentence, this Hebrew of the Hebrews shows his appreciation of the Greek ideal of *paideia* in its strength and, here without any hint of Christian imperialism, sees it as part of what faith can use for its upbuilding into maturity.[12] This should make Western Christians today ashamed that they do not make better use of and derive more enjoyment from all the privileges which they possess. Professional ministers must bear their share of the blame for this because they have not insisted sufficiently to the rich communities they serve that wealth without faith, including wealth produced as the fruit of faith, engenders anxiety and anxiety provokes greed and the abuse of wealth, and the abuse of wealth creates envy and a spirit of emulation, which issue in ugliness and misery. It is small consolation to observe that the academic community may be even more to blame. Here, more than in its churches, society has poured its wealth since the war and it is here, above all, that life in the creation should be celebrated with delight but it sometimes seems that here is where people have developed the greatest expertise in making themselves and each other unnecessarily miserable. One of the things which used to strike me most forcibly when I began to visit the USA from war-ravaged Europe, and which endeared the since much-abused American way of life to most of the rest of the world, was the unaffected good humour of the people, as they honestly enjoyed life in a good place, a quality which shone through all the meretricious gloss even of old Hollywood films. One of the few justifications for the existence in their present form of the phenomenally prosperous suburban churches which are such a feature of the USA, whose deficiencies as a false abstraction from the totality of the life of the community America's internal critics so faithfully castigate, has been that they are, at least, singularly happy communities. If they have done nothing else, they have helped to build up the world's poor stock of that surplus good temper and nervous energy and material resource which have given some people strength, and the magnanimity which comes from strength, to help face and overcome the difficulties of less privileged places.

3

The Temptations of Maturity

To say what was said about American life at the end of the last
chapter is not, of course, to tell the whole story. In particular, it
should be carefully noted that this everyday cheerfulness is part of
the overflow of Christian maturity rather than the expression of what
lies at its heart. Perhaps it is an American heresy, reflected in the
bland, ever-smiling countenance of some of its sects, to place it at the
heart. Yet provided Americans realize, as some of those who coined
the phrases may not have done, that a country must have its roots
very deep in grace before its members can see it as actually 'self-
evident' that people have 'an inalienable right' to the 'pursuit of happiness', they have cause for celebration that they belong to such a
country.

This is the kind of proviso which the joyful pages of the New
Testament have always to be making. The richer we are, the more
cause for celebration we have, the more vulnerable we become. The
higher we rise, the further we fall. Lucifer was one of the greatest of
the angels and, we are told, 'from dawn to dewey eve he fell, a
summer's day'. This is why the temptations of maturity are more
deadly than those of childhood and adolescence and why, with growing maturity, vigilance must increase and not be relaxed. Again, it is
noteworthy that the letter to the Ephesians, which develops so richly
the way in which the spirit of Christ enables us to realize the fullness
of humanity in a cosmic setting, has to end with an appeal to put on
the whole armour which God provides if we are to stand firm in our
exalted position against all the onslaughts of the devil. To the extent
that we grow into the fullness of the stature of Christ, we make a very
large target. This is why a discussion of the qualities of maturity has
to be followed immediately by a reminder of its temptations.

The first of these arises directly out of the new-found strength which liberation engenders. To the outward eye, as one human being among others, no one is more autonomous, more 'inner-directed' and independent of external authority than the person who possesses faith. He is the veritable master of his fate and captain of his soul. Paul is Christ's bond-servant but, as he frequently has to remind the obstreperous Corinthians, that does not mean that he is anyone else's bond-servant except when Christ commands him to be, and the authority he possesses from Christ is not to be overridden. He was acutely aware, however, of the dangers of this position and, as his tortured convolutions in the second letter to the Corinthians so movingly reveal, he is at pains to avoid appearing to 'boast' because of this. It is said of Calvin that he feared God always but man never. That is the authentic independence of Christian maturity and it is a quality in short supply in the nervous Christian community today. The trouble is that such attitudes give those who possess them a great deal of power and when someone finds that his fearlessness leads others to go in fear of him, it is hard to remember that he is meant to be of gentle spirit and easy to exploit the situation in order to dictate to others what they should do for their own good. From this it is a short step to conclude that one is a strong person in one's own right, who does not need to fear God either, and to congratulate oneself on one's own unconquerable soul.

The sin of pride is a familiar enough theme of Christian moralists[1] but it has not always been seen how much it is a sin of advanced maturity and, therefore, how extremely subtle and insidious its operations are. Modern theology, aided by some elements in existentialist psychology, has exposed the way in which one can succumb to the pride of reason by showing that the range of experience within which one can be trusted to use reason honestly is much more circumscribed than most forms of rationalism will admit. It has not been so alert in showing that spiritual pride can be even more damaging. The cruder forms of a 'holier-than-thou' attitude are readily detectable, not least when they express themselves in that false humility already mentioned. What is harder to discern, and still harder for anyone else to point out to the culprit, is the pride which arises from a serious attempt to be faithful to a difficult vocation, especially when it is unpopular and misunderstood. All spiritual vocation is costly, and it makes demands on others closely involved as well as on the person called, but it is very easy for the one called to dramatize himself as the only faithful one and to develop the attitudes of a superior person, especially when the others show signs of stumbling under the weight of the burden he has caused to be laid upon them.[2]

The line between dedication and self-importance is very fine, and the very devotion that a successful leader inspires can encourage him to cross it. Jesus had to face this danger in his third temptation and it is one reason why he is so emphatic that the true leader must take the form of a servant. His recognition of this is what distinguishes the mature Christian from the 'charismatic' cult-figure. He has nothing within him of the egotism of the romantic artist, who sacrifices others, especially members of the other sex, to his own conception of the exigencies of his genius, nor does he have the spirit of the tycoon, who incorporates the bones of his victims in monuments to his own glory. Yet he will also know how near at hand attitudes like these are, especially when he is confronted by the claims of rivals to spiritual authority. This is what makes Paul's insight in II Corinthians so remarkable, when he has to assert his apostolic authority and resist attempts to undermine it while at the same time trying to avoid self-aggrandisement and to retain the basis for making peace with those who are attacking him.

Paul is hardly less aware of the next danger, which arises from pride, and that is complacency. He shows this in his bitterly sarcastic contrast, in the fourth chapter of the first letter to them, between the Corinthian *phronimoi*, the wiseacres, 'such successful Christians' as the New English Bible calls them, and the apostles themselves, who are like the scum of the earth. Again, it is necessary to see how it is success itself which breeds complacency, and success which is the fruit of genuine faith. If one has ventured into the unknown, risking all in the leap of faith, floating on seventy thousand fathoms, and finds one's faith vindicated, what then? Having first sought God's kingdom and his righteousness, in due season one finds that the good things of this life also are added unto one. It would be pusillanimous and ungrateful not to enjoy them but it quickly becomes the easiest thing in the world to assume that they are one's natural birthright and that nothing more is required than to go on enjoying them.

No one has described more vividly the radicalism of the leap of faith than Søren Kierkegaard in his book *Fear and Trembling*,[3] as he reflects upon the significance of the Genesis story of Abraham and God's demand that he sacrifice his son Isaac. What he does not do is to face the question of what happens after Isaac has been handed back to Abraham and the old man is faced with all the problems of the boy's upbringing. The difficulties he would have had to deal with would have been more complex, if not more intense, than those which confronted him in his test, both because Isaac would seem even more precious to him after the immense agony of having to raise the knife to kill him and because it would seem to be only reasonable that he was now free simply to enjoy his son in his own old age. Yet the later history of Israel stands to make clear that this would have been insufficient.

This infinitely rich story suggests another way in which complacency frequently creeps in, a way which is a warning against the trivialization of spiritual temptation. This trivialization can easily lead those who consider themselves to be spiritually 'serious' to assume that, because they are not likely to succumb to it in its obvious forms, therefore this, at least, must be a temptation from which they can claim immunity. Suppose Isaac, in his turn, becomes aware of the cost at which his life has been won, and now understanding both the greatness of his father's love towards himself and his greater love for God, realizes how infinitely precious his heritage is and how heavy a responsibility he has to maintain it. In the most admirable way he becomes a conservative, because it is possible even to become a conservative guardian of the radicalism of faith – forgetting, as we all do, that no one has the courage to be genuinely radical except in an existential situation where, like Abraham, he is left with no alternative. The more he finds others to be ignorant of the meaning of that heritage, perhaps even so completely missing the point as to denounce his father as the murderer of his own child, the more determinedly defensive he is driven to be. But this inexorably means that he becomes more interested in his past than in his future. The powerful influence of religious nostalgia begins its work, nostalgia which is all the more powerful the greater the radicalism of faith out of which the heritage was created. This means that his horizons begin to contract and what lies ahead, with all the changes it will bring, seems increasingly threatening. He forgets that the fulfilment of the promise to his father still lies in the future and that he has his own part to play, on the same terms, in its realization. He ceases to be a pilgrim and becomes content to remain where he is, making the most of what he has and the thought of raising the knife to kill his own children makes him recoil with horror. Thus complacency is born, at the very point where the fruit of living faith is being gathered. The implication of this for the church's self-understanding are obvious.

The next step in the progression away from living faith is sloth. Karl Barth, in volumes IV.1 and IV.2 respectively of his *Church*

Dogmatics, has two long chapters on the pride of man and the sloth of man, and there is an obvious connection between the two. Those of his critics who argue that he exalts the function of the theologian unduly might be disposed to hint that he has not escaped the first sin but even the sternest of them, contemplating the vast scope and size of *Church Dogmatics* could hardly charge him with the other, so that his words on the subject have extra authority. He analyses sloth under the headings of stupidity, and that indifference to one's neighbour which issues in inhumanity, of the dissipation which is the sign of loss of control and of the worry which arises because one knows that one is failing to fulfil one's vocation and lacks the energy to do anything about it. He produces a series of vivid Old Testament examples of these different aspects of sloth which make excellent starting points for pastoral sermons on the subject. He also brings out what we have seen to be true in relation to pride and complacency, that these are often corruptions of virtues and can sometimes masquerade as such. Thus he argues, a little surprisingly, that sloth can hide itself behind an appearance of worldly wisdom. Barth particularly emphasizes, as one might expect, that the Christian on the road to maturity is an active man, a pilgrim, who is concerned to keep moving towards his destination. Spiritual food is given him to sustain him on the journey, manna in the wilderness, sufficient for one day in one place. If, however, through pride and complacency, he becomes content to stay where he is, he begins to fall out of condition and to lose his appetite. The prospect of moving becomes increasingly unattractive and he uses his energy chiefly to find excuses for inactivity, concentrating much more on the delights of the flesh than on the food of the spirit, and yet the prey of futile worry because he knows that these are not enough to satisfy him. This is what leads him, although Barth does not mention it at this particular point in his discussion, to the restless search for novelty, as a distraction, a way of passing the time when he has lost the preoccupations of the journey. This is the characteristic vice of old and tired civilizations, of cities which have become secularized waste lands as they have cut themselves off from the sources of renewal.

If, in a broad generalization, worry, with its concomitant of neurosis, might be described as the characteristic northern and Protestant consequence of sloth, passivity, the listless, unreflective repetition of routine, is the characteristic southern and Catholic and Orthodox consequence of sloth. This latter is an even more advanced form of retreat from Christian maturity.[4] It is important that, in both its

25

forms, this sloth be recognized for what it is, so that its causes, rather than merely its symptoms, should receive treatment. There may, for example, be no point in continuing to do what earnest practitioners have been trying to do for a long time, to pump more and more spiritual food into those who suffer from sloth in the hope that they can be stirred into action. If they can no longer digest it or burn it up in creative energy, it will only make them fatter and slower than they were before, using even the masterpieces of the Christian past as mere distractions, switching them on and off between yawns. How best to deal with this situation is a matter for discussion. A period of enforced starvation, which compels them again to see the value of what they had taken for granted, may be the only way out for many, but even that does not always produce the desired result and to try to bring it about, when we are surrounded by such riches which could be of great benefit to us if they were properly used, is a tempting of God. What is beyond dispute is that, in a situation like this, it is essential that the Christian community should see that its shape in the world is meant to be determined by the way in which it tries to express the qualities of maturity and to avoid the vices of pride, complacency and sloth which can easily arise as defects of those qualities, so that its members can continue to keep moving towards their goal.

4

Men, Women and Maturity

Christian maturity has to be expressed in all parts of life and this is true of intimate personal relations no less than of the general life of the church. In some ways, its nature should be most clearly visible here because our actions are more directly under our own control and the problems inherent in the existence of all institutions less obtrusive. Yet, just because we are so involved personally, it is here also that the difficulties can be at their most acute.

To consider first a matter which is of almost obsessive preoccupation in Western countries today, that of relations between men and women. That the preoccupation has this obsessive quality is one of the signs that the times are out of joint. It will not be removed until the Christian community has shown more imaginative insight into the subject than it has so far been able to find.

This is not to imply that all elements in the preoccupation are unhealthy. It has arisen partly as a consequence of the greatly enhanced self-consciousness and sense of individuality which have long been characteristics of the modern world but to which women have only recently taken the opportunity to give expression as well as men. In this situation, we are fortunate in having a classic Christian statement of what this individuality means, one which takes the measure of what it involves. Admittedly, it is written by a man but by a man who, as we shall see, had the deepest respect for this individuality in women also. Kierkegaard believed that it was his vocation to work out as fully as possible what it means to be the self-conscious individual before God, as seriously as Descartes did but with a more active awareness of what God's providential rule means and always with the knowledge that individuality has ultimately to find its fulfilment in community, in the realization of the universal human.[1] It is in this context that we must consider the significance of his action in breaking his engagement to marry Regine Olsen, the young girl whom he loved and who loved him. The banal reductionism of those who try to explain it away on the basis of some physical or psychic defect can be dismissed out of hand by anyone who has taken the trouble to read anything Kierkegaard wrote about personal relationships. We can safely take it that he meant what he said when he related it to his vocation to explore what it means to be the individual and that he lacked confidence that both he and Regine possessed the spiritual resources to maintain that vocation in the married state. 'If I had had enough faith, I would have remained with Regine.' It was evidence of his fundamental maturity, of his recognition that full humanity is co-humanity. He knew that his destiny was to realize the universal human and that it was the aim of the reflective person to achieve maturity on a profounder level than is possible without reflection, but he was afraid that he could not trust himself to maintain the tension involved in faithfulness to his vocation unless he could rely on the understanding co-operation of his partner. It was not that he was worried that he and Regine would not be happy together but that they would find happiness too readily on a superficial level and forget their vocation. His nightmare was that they might end up like Frederic and Juliana, the complacently domesticated couple in their cosy country parsonage whom he satirized with increasing bitterness as he grew older. It is a pity that we never had Regine's side of the story, expressed with something approaching the self-consciousness and power of articulation of Søren. We might have learnt something of the way in which those who have a highly developed sense of individuality and those who have the gift of achieving spontaneity more simply and directly, without having to make herculean creative efforts to get themselves out of the way, can complement each other and build each other up. And if they had been able to marry Søren, with his incomparable genius, might have been able to give us that account of the true inwardness of the marriage relationship which the Christian community badly needs in these confused and unhappy times. He might also have given us that fresh light on how to bring up the children of the covenant, upon whom the burden of individuality lies so heavily, which we need hardly less badly. It was not to be and, in this slackly hedonistic age, we are left only to admire the superb restraint and tenderness which Søren showed in resisting the temptation to have less than a full marriage in the way he understood it with the Regine he dearly loved, for her sake as much as his own. He was no Byron or Wagner, and he spared Regine the kind of tortured Scandinavian marriage which Ibsen or Ingmar Bergmann would have loved to delineate.

We have to do without Kierkegaard's celebration of the relationship between man and woman, therefore, but we do, at least, have Karl Barth's extensive treatment of the subject.[2] This lacks the concentration, the wit and the elegance of style of Kierkegaard, its exegesis of the second creation story in Genesis is more free than modern scholarship will allow and there is one important place where I should want to put the emphasis very differently, but his treatment has the merit of discussing the subject in the context of Christian maturity and it makes some fundamental points with great clarity.

The first of these is his insistence that humanity is co-humanity. On the face of it, that might seem to be so obvious in this context as not to be worth saying. That 'man is for the woman made and the woman for the man', in the words of the old song, is hardly an original insight. Yet because our estrangement from ourselves means the distortion of relationships on the most basic levels, it is here that things begin to go most wrong, and Barth brings this out very clearly by his imaginative treatment of the second creation story. The damage goes right back to the roots, and true radicalism means a re-examination of the roots. And being so deep-rooted, this is the hardest relationship to set right. Barth's point is that to see that humanity is co-humanity is an insight which, in our fallen state, we can only properly apprehend by grace coming from outside ourselves.

It is not surprising, therefore, that most of the temptations of success which afflict the Christian life are as active in relations between men and women in their distinctiveness as anywhere else and that they need the presence of all the virtues of maturity if they are to be overcome. Even in Christian circles, people have become so preoccupied with the sexual aspects of this relationship that its other temptations, and its other hopeful possibilities, have not received sufficient attention. The sexual aspect cannot, of course, be overlooked — as though there were any danger of that happening in these days — but many sexual problems are intensified because attitudes are wrong on other levels. Most of us have to get ourselves out of the way before we can discover each other, and in the process our common maturity, and the more self-conscious we are the more this matters. It is another strength of Barth's discussion that, with his characteristic theological courage, he says that the main Christian argument in favour of monogamy is that it brings out most clearly the commitment involved in uniquely and honestly personal choice.

It is the best human analogy to the way in which God has chosen us. This is the place on earth where liberation, as the Christian understands it, finds its best expression, in an act of responsible choice which inevitably carries with it an explicit limitation in other directions if the reciprocity which is integral to the relationship is to be achieved.

The great objection to notions of free love, which have a recurring fascination for some Christian heretics and which are having one of their periodic revivals today, is that they fail to do justice to the way in which freedom has to express itself in this context. The degree of commitment which the relationship demands from both parties is such that all the spiritual resources available for this aspect of their lives are needed for its fulfillment. It may, perhaps, be theoretically possible for more than two people to have such a relationship with each other simultaneously but the possibilities of self and mutual deception are so infinite and the vulnerability of the partners to being wounded by each other so great, that a measure of sanctity would be required on all sides for which most of us have to wait until the world to come, where, we are reliably informed, there is neither marrying nor giving in marriage. The very limitation involved in the act of commitment in marriage is itself part of the paradigm of how freedom works in co-humanity.[3] It does this not least because experience proves that it gives that release from self-preoccupation which enables those who accept it to act with a new kind of detached goodwill to others. It is those who know marriage in this way who find it easiest to be of gentle spirit, peacemakers, generous, magnanimous and joyful, although it is also true that, as we might expect, they also find it easier to succumb to pride, complacency and sloth.

Where Barth in the *Dogmatics* is open to criticism is at a surprising place, given his characteristic emphasis in theology and all the remarkable insights he has to offer about the nature of time. He does not see the relationship between men and women sufficiently in an eschatological context. This may be partly because, in the way he chose to make his exposition unfold, he dealt with ethics so extensively under the heading of the doctrine of creation,[4] but it has a regrettable consequence. Because he concentrates so much on the Genesis story, remarkably positive as his interpretation of it may be, he has to give undue weight to the notions of masculine precedence and feminine subordination. Paul before him had to do the same, but with more excuse. The Genesis story may faithfully reflect the way in which we have evolved but, even when it is given the Christian interpretation Barth provides, it remains an account of what is past.[5] And as Barth himself would be among the first to insist, it is what lies ahead which matters most for the follower of Christ. The nature of our co-humanity is not determined by the creation story but by what we know of God in Christ, and Christ is more than what is recorded for us of the man Jesus. He is the exalted Christ, who now calls us forward in the Spirit. To quote I John: 'Beloved, we are God's children now; and it does not yet appear what we shall be, but we know that when he appears we shall be like him, for we shall see him as he is.'[6] The pointers which the Spirit gives concerning the nature of that life emphasizes its equality and mutuality,[7] and it is this which should determine our relationships here and now, rather than any orders of precedence which are projected forward from past experience and whose relevance diminishes the more we move forward in our new life.

What implications does this have? First, because men and women have a common calling as children of God, with all the concomitants for maturity which we have tried to see, especially in relation to freedom, choice and responsibility, it is not at this fundamental level that any differences between men and women can have significance. As Barth himself says, any attempt to differentiate masculine and feminine principles at this level can be nothing other than dangerously misleading. Those women who fight to maintain the recognition in practice of the principle that this freedom is inherent in our humanity and not the prerogative of the members of one sex are fighting the battle of all, and it is a matter of deep shame to the Christian community that it has so often to be fought on Christian soil. Humanity is co-humanity. We are ourselves only in relationship and all are impoverished if the full freedom and responsibility of some is denied, and this is especially true of the most fundamental of relationships.

Secondly, this common calling does not remove the differences between men and women, any more for that matter than it removes the differences between members of the same sex, but it does determine the way in which they are to be dealt with. As Barth finely puts it, the differences prompt us to consider one another, hear the question which each puts to the other and make responsible answer to one another.[8] We cannot ignore the differences. We are unsettled by them, so that there is an inescapable tension in our dealings with each other. They pose the question concerning our humanity as we meet it in a different form from that which we know in ourselves, although

Barth does not discuss the problem of the exact way in which this question differs when it concerns the relationship between men and women from when it concerns any relationship with another person. Where he comes near to doing so, he is likely to arouse a good deal of controversy in these days because he maintains the traditional position that the relationship between men and women is controlled by a definite order, in which man precedes woman.

In saying this, Barth shows uncharacteristic concern to safeguard himself against misunderstanding. He does not want this to be taken in any crudely male chauvinist way and he is at pains to emphasize that the mutuality of the relationship must be understood in a fully Christian sense. 'Man speaks against himself', he says in his earlier treatment of the same theme, 'if he assesses and treats woman as an inferior being for without her weakness and subsequence he would not be man. And woman speaks against herself if she envies that which is proper to man, for his strength and precedence are the reality without which she could not be woman.'[9] In fairness to Barth, that quotation, with its references to weakness and subsequence may be misleading. He himself issues a warning against giving theological weight to secondary male and female characteristics which are relative, historically conditioned and stand in need of constant critical scrutiny. We can be confident that, despite his Swiss citizenship, he would have been on the side of campaigners for women's rights over many of the issues for which they fight. The question remains, however, as to how far it is appropriate any longer to think of relations between men and women in terms of strength and weakness and precedence and subsequence, let alone of superiority and inferiority. And by 'any longer' I do not refer to the second half of the twentieth century, as though any special insight has been given to us denied to our forebears. I refer to the Christian dispensation as a whole, where what we are to become, not what we have been, must be determinative. With all its limitations, the Pauline teaching about relations between men and women, like the practice of Jesus, represented an advance on current practice of the time. The question is whether we have continued to make the progress inherent in the basic insights of our faith or whether we have fallen back.

This is a large matter, and it would be foolish to rush in with a conclusion, especially as the atmosphere of the present time is not conducive to taking cool looks at this subject in a long perspective. Let me simply say this, which will, I hope, be taken as evidence of my good faith in relation to the fundamental equality of men and women in co-humanity. We shall be in a better position to evaluate what truth and error, and continuing relevance for the present situation, there is in the admittedly biblical notion of masculine precedence when we have an analysis of the notion by a woman theologian which shows an insight and grasp of first principles at least comparable to that of Barth.[10] It should be added that masculine theologians stand in need of such a study as much as women do, for the sake of their competence at their own jobs, because without it they will not define co-humanity in this sphere aright and have to face the possibility that they may have a large number of words to eat. Until such a work appears, no theological judgments should be made which assume the self-evident truth of this notion because it is found in scripture and tradition.

Thirdly, and related to this, there is no other subject than this where it is more appropriate, and more important, that the Christian community should conduct its discussion according to its own highest standards of civility. Obstinate masculine conservatism and militant feminism are equally out of place, although there may be more excuse for the latter than the former. Here, above all, the virtues of maturity should be receiving their clearest expression, the gentleness of spirit which expresses itself in tenderness and readiness to listen, the peace-making without which a true home cannot come into being, generosity which puts the most positive interpretation on the difficulties and aspirations of the other, the magnanimity which is tolerant and forgiving when people believe that they have been wounded by sexual discrimination, and above all joy. In so far as women succeed in expressing more fully the liberation which is already our common possession in Christ, this should be an occasion for celebration, to men as well as to themselves. Since humanity is co-humanity, we shall all be enriched by it.[11] Surely in these matters above all others it is the denial of our faith to treat each other as opponents and we do not have to speak of them to each other as though we were foreigners, those of strange tongue, and not fellow members of the house of Israel.

This becomes the more important to remember when we realize that if there are to be changes in the respective roles of men and women in the family and in the wider life of society, this demands greater understanding and mutual respect between them, not less. If, for example, a woman wishes to start or to renew a career in middle life after concentrating for many years on her home and children, this imposes a fresh strain both upon her and her husband, at a time

33

when marriages are in any case often vulnerable. Here, as elsewhere, relationships need to deepen as their range grows. Christians in these days are, of course, much disturbed by the problems created by marital breakdown, increasingly within the heart of the Christian community itself, but we have still not paid enough attention to what maturity in marriage involves, nor set our sights high enough for what we might expect successful life-long marriage to achieve, nor drawn sufficiently on the resources which are available to help towards its fulfilment by overcoming pride, complacency and sloth.

This may also help to re-establish, or where necessary to create, civilized conventions of behaviour in other relationships than those of marriage. Here also the temptations as well as the virtues of maturity need to be borne particularly in mind, because we are easily able to deceive each other, and sometimes ourselves. This is obviously especially true in relations between men and women who have not reached the point of marital commitment. One of the marks of a mature Christian community should be that it has well-defined and yet subtle and sensitive courting conventions, which try to safeguard the seriousness and the mystery of commitment by providing people with plenty of opportunities to deepen their knowledge of each other while, at the same time, laying emphasis on the restraint which is a barrier to exploitation and allowing ways of graceful withdrawal without causing avoidable wounds. We have served our children ill in this generation by not fighting harder to retain what seemly conventions existed in this area, leaving them to work out conventions of their own in a cruel world, where the cynical standards of commercial hucksters reign or where they have little protection against the harsh conformisms of their short-sighted peer groups in college or bed-sitter land.

High standards and clear conventions over marriage and what leads up to it will also help restore civility to other relationships which have suffered impoverishment. This is particularly true of friendship, where excessive self-consciousness about the sexual element which might be one factor among others in it, have made people nervous and inhibited. One of the advantages of the rigidity of convention in relation to marriage and sexual expression which prevailed in Christian circles in Victorian times, uncharitably as it may sometimes have been maintained, was that it liberated people to show the warmth of affection in other relationships of life, towards relatives and children and friends of either sex without the fear of being misunderstood. Christians should show indignation at the way in which literary nosey parkers grub away at the details of private lives of our forebears in the hope of finding some dirt in a corner, which they then proudly display before the gaze of every passer-by, meanwhile protesting that, of course, from their enlightened point of view, it is not dirt. Maturity should give us the confidence not to be deterred by the pseudo-tolerance of the prurient from expressing healthy natural affection in ways appropriate to the level of commitment involved in the relationship. It is an impoverished society indeed where friends and colleagues, whether of the same or the other sex, are embarrassed about being seen much in each other's company because of what people might say, or where only the potential dangers, and none of the beauty, of the love of bachelors and spinsters for young children, are dwelt upon. It is not Lewis Carroll but those who write about him in such terms who see anything sinister in the affectionately humorous and utterly unsentimental observation which he bestows on Alice. Victorian standards were far from ideal, and they were often severely damaged by undue class consciousness, but the very zeal with which their limitations and hypocrisies have been documented by their successors suggests that all has not been progress since their time. Quite apart from what is happening in the world around us, a new effort to set itself higher standards of maturity in these matters is required by the Christian community itself.

5

Youth and Age

The observations just made about the Victorians have a measure of truth also in the sphere where they were considered by many who came after them to be even less successful than in dealing with relations between the sexes; the sphere of relationships between parents and children and, more broadly, between age and youth. The typical Victorians saw clearly enough the need to train their children in the acceptance of responsibility and also realized the importance of passing on the best of their own experience, by precept and example supported by strong conventions. They saw life, as all mature societies must, in a perspective longer than that of one generation. What many of them did not see so clearly was how success, and the power it brings, can corrupt even the most high-minded, nor did they readily appreciate the problems which arise for the children of the successful if they are to arrive at their own maturity.

The story of Abraham and Isaac has already been referred to and I have always regarded it as one of the confirmations of the divine inspiration of scripture that it emerged from the mists of antiquity at the very beginning of the history of Israel. The point is missed unless we see that Abraham's trial befell him to warn him of the dangers of success. He is the archetype of the rich man, the one blessed by God, and it is in Isaac, through whom alone the covenant promise is to be fulfilled, that all his riches are concentrated. Some aspects of the significance of the demand that Abraham sacrifice Isaac for the church's understanding of her vocation have already been discussed. It is no less significant for relations within the natural family. For Abraham to have set his love of Isaac above God would have been to stunt Isaac, making him over into Abraham's image and thus preventing him from achieving his own maturity, turning him into the conservative described in our third chapter. It is only when

Abraham has achieved the inner detachment which makes him see that he must not get in the way of Isaac's own relation with God that he becomes fit to be entrusted with Isaac's upbringing.

Isaac remains the heir and has to carry on the tradition, but Abraham can prepare him for this without falling into the error of either paternalism or maternalism, if these slightly dubious metaphorical terms are not entirely inappropriate. The danger of the former, which was particularly acute in Victorian Britain, is that the child will be kept too long in a subordinate position. He is given the advantage of a disciplined upbringing and he is trained to expect to make his own judgments and carry responsibility, but his father may be so anxious that the child should follow in his own footsteps and may be so sure that he knows best that the child is denied the freedom to make his own judgments and exercise responsibility. But if paternalism is the characteristic danger of successful old-established societies, families and businesses, maternalism is that of successful new ones, as well as of those which are reacting against the excessive paternalism of their own parents. The parents will have worked so hard for success in their own terms that they have little time and imagination left with which to enjoy it. They want to do it through their children. The result is that, as we say, they 'spoil' them, while at the same time laying the burden of great expectations upon them. Not only must they carry on the success of their parents but their success, in ways the parents can enjoy, must be more spectacular, since through the efforts of their parents they have so many more advantages. Yet to the extent that they have been 'spoiled', they lack the training to reach their own maturity. If, nevertheless, they manage to do so, it will be in ways which disconcert and disappoint their parents. Either way, as recent experience in much of Western society proves, mutual misunderstanding and frustration are likely to follow and an unhealthily large 'gap' between the generations emerges.

An English sociologist, Frank Musgrove, wrote a book in the early sixties called *Youth and the Social Order*, in which he argued that higher education was a conspiracy to mould young people to fulfil a subordinate role for as long as possible and keep them out of competition with their elders. It was a development of the concept of adolescence[1] which was invented for that very reason round about the same time as the steam engine, with all the new social implications that industrialization brought. This is a tendentious half-truth.[2] Adolescence is also a consequence of a more highly developed sense of individuality and higher education, and the period of study, reflection and controlled irresponsibility which it provides is an invaluable aid in reaching independence of judgment and a higher level of maturity than would otherwise be possible in an increasingly complex society. Yet this half-truth has the merit of shaking the complacency of the academic community, with its characteristic assumption that the kind of higher education it offers is always self-evidently a good thing and its tendency to ignore the extent of its dependence on attitudes taken for granted in the wider community to which it belongs. When people in that wider community no longer possess strong convictions of their own and leave the next generation to work out its own salvation, soothing their consciences by making available to it the resources of higher education while retaining real power for themselves, many of the conditions for the creation of an alienated generation are present. The leaders of the academic community, by the policy of heedless expansion without reference to wider social considerations which they have pursued in several Western lands over the last generation, cannot escape some of the responsibility for the creation of such conditions.

In another recent book, *Saeculum: History and Society in the Theology of St Augustine*,[3] Dr R. A. Markus, helps us to see the relation between youth and age in a different perspective. He points out that when the ancients wanted an example of weakness, they took it not from age but from youth. Weak adults produce vulnerable children and they realized that children are particularly exposed to contagious diseases. The longer they are kept as children, *in statu pupillari*, the more virulent the disease becomes, just as measles and chicken pox are more damaging in late youth than in early childhood. All this suggests that, instead of echoing the noisiest cries of pain of those who are suffering in these ways, or of providing them only with tea and sympathy, Christians concerned with growth toward maturity would be better employed in asking whether we have got the balance and the timing between minority and majority right. All institutions become possessive and like to keep their children in the nest for too long. We shall see that this is true of churches. It may be that this is now more urgently true of institutions of higher education. They are unlikely to find a satisfactory answer unless they are submitted to unwelcome pressure from outside themselves.

Real freedom for those who come after us means the ability to look into the unknown for themselves and there take their own decisions. Success for their parents comes only when they are able to do so on their parent's shoulders, seeing further than they would have been able to do without their help. If those who carry the burdens of maturity find that they are unable to walk upright as they do so,[4] the range of the vision of their children will inevitably be narrowed. The difficulties which many of the most apparently privileged young people in the Western world experience today suggests that the fault may well lie as much with the immaturity of their parents as with their own.

If our immaturity is causing problems to our children, it may also be building up difficulties for ourselves, and for our immediate predecessors, as we move into old age. The next group who are likely to be the victims of the uncertainty and confused guilt-feelings of the liberally minded are the aged. This has already begun to happen in Britain. As with all groups who suffer this fate, they do so because, in relation to them, those who should be acting in a mature way have a great deal about which to feel guilty. Many of them have lost the perspective on life which enables them to give dignity to old age and their hedonism can find no place for those who cannot contribute to their pleasure or even fend for themselves. Yet, as with pre-maturity, even efforts to redress this situation can make it worse if an inadequate response to the challenge of maturity leads people to a wrong conception of what post-maturity should be like, speaking of post-maturity here in relation to the natural life-cycle.

The danger is that, in compensation for past failures, old people are encouraged to become primarily the recipients of charity and thus over-dependent, with the consequence that their own maturity is diminished and the advent of second childhood is hastened. Here above all, we need to beware of Christians when they come bearing gifts. Those who, like myself, are themselves drawing near to old age should take the initiative, while there is still time, in working out a different approach.

First, as they grow older they should organize their lives so as to ensure that they remain active and useful as long as possible, while at the same time continuing to be aware that the virtues and the temptations of maturity can still be present. What is vital is that the inner detachment be maintained which enables them to see that the worst way to keep useful as well as active is by clinging to responsibility and power which are now more appropriately exercised by others. Continuing maturity is best demonstrated by the voluntary surrender of these before the point is reached when their possessors themselves feel that they are becoming too much for them. This is unlikely to become clear to them before it is clear to their colleagues. They should also have the good sense to know that, if they are to undertake new responsibilities, more suited to advancing years and declining powers, they will need all the energy they still feel for making the necessary adjustments and starting their new tasks with zest. People are likely to be more effective in their sixties if they stop going on trying increasingly hard to do what was appropriate for them in their forties or fifties, and they are probably able to continue to be useful for much longer.

But secondly, it matters a great deal that these changes be made with due respect for the dignity of old age. This is more than a matter of softening the impact of painful change, although since we shall all have to go this way one day we have a common interest in doing this. It is one of creating the conditions in which older people can make their best contribution. The graceful phasing out from responsibility should be as high an art in a civilized community as the phasing into it over which we seem to have such difficulty today. The prophet speaks of the young having visions and the old dreaming dreams. Visions refer to as yet unrealized possibilities; dreams to illuminating re-organizations of past experience. As the young mature and try to implement their visions, the old can provide correctives and amendments to their efforts and do so without, however, having the power and responsibility to carry them through, which would mean the inevitable distortion of the vision. It is the practice in Britain to elevate superannuated politicians and other public servants to the House of Lords, where much of what they do is exactly that. The excessive archaism and pomp of the House of Lords do not commend it as a model, but this aspect of its function might be more widely copied. It would be easiest to start with professional groups which have a good deal of freedom to reorganize themselves along these lines.[5] This might help throw light on how to approach the much more difficult problems of those who face old age with little formal education and with skills diminishing rapidly because they are based on physical capacity. One of the insufficiently considered costs of our over-industrialized and over-mechanized society is that old age is much harder to bear than it used to be in traditional society for those who have had to carry some of its heaviest burdens. The freedom to watch television is a poor substitute for freedom from loneliness and loss of function.

Three considerations should govern a Christian approach to this matter. First, the importance of building up resources for meeting the demands of post-maturity while we still have the strength of maturity must be emphasized. This means more than the sensible cultivation of interests and hobbies which can be carried through into retirement. It is a matter of the way in which one spends one's whole life, so that one has a fund of memories and generous reflections which can sustain one's spirit in solitude and sleeplessness or illness. Since the memories of childhood seem to recur with special vividness in old age, a rich childhood has special importance. One of the sad things about many people today as they face old age is the poverty of their inner life in youth and maturity. The fact that most of us live longer than our forebears did means that our earlier development should be fuller and stronger. It is not always evident that this is so.

Secondly, the support of the wider community is, if anything, even more necessary in old age than earlier, not merely for material help but also for giving the stimulus to continuing activity. It is a common complaint, especially in an old country like Britain, that the churches fail to capture the loyalty of the young. This is understandable but it sometimes prevents us from seeing that the old also need evangelism. This is not necessarily because, as they near their journey's end, people become more interested in what lies beyond than in the passing scene. Observation suggests that it is usually only those who have been alive to that question at other stages in their journey who are able to raise it with enough existential intensity to hope to receive any fresh answers at a time when their imagination and critical faculties are in decline, although bereavement may sometimes bestir them. It is rather that people need to be called out of their isolation and gathered into a community which serves a purpose greater than their own as much when they are old, when it is so easy to slip into self-centred isolation, as when they are younger. Any service they do must be realistically related to their capacities and sensitively linked with what those coming after them are doing, and this demands unsentimental honesty and frankness on both sides, but there is no reason why it should not be genuinely creative. It could be that in the period which succeeds that of Christendom, if ours is indeed a post-Christendom age, it would be to the old rather than to the young that one would look most hopefully for guidance. When the world is tired and vision seems to have faded, those with the longest memories and the fullest experience of life may be better able to draw on the wisdom of the past to help in the present. And those few who have maintained their vigilance with such alertness that, as they draw near to it, they could have fresh insight into eternity, may also be able to tell us what matters most about the future.

Thirdly, it follows from this that there must be much more inter-change between people at the various stages of life than is customary in modern society. The rule that we all need each other, and the best of each other, holds throughout the whole of life. Obviously the old, like everyone else, need institutions and facilities which cater for their special needs, and this is particularly true of the very old and the handicapped. And we have already emphasized that they will be scrupulous, even to the point of being over-scrupulous, not to get in the way, and therefore in the light, of those who are younger. But there must be relationship as well as differentiation and the whole community suffers when there is disproportionate segregation. The young need to see people ageing with dignity and gathering the fruits in their lives of an earlier period than their own. They also need to be reminded of dissolution and death, and of the need to come to terms with bereavement. And, as we have said, the old need, in due but not excessive measure, the stimulus of the fresh approach to life of the young. Humanity is co-humanity and that is true between people at life's various stages as well as between men and women. When only one stage of life is taken into account and regarded as the norm, all is distorted. Christian maturity enables us to act our age, at whatever stage of the natural cycle we may happen to be, but it does so only by teaching us how much we depend upon each other, right through. When it does, it can provide us with some of life's most satisfying experiences. For an old person to pretend to act like a young one is unseemly, but nothing is more beautiful than to see old people stimulated by the young into a vitality which enables them to handle the possibilities of their present situation in such a way as to give the young a glimpse of what they must have been like in their youth. Nothing, that is, unless it is for the old to see emerging in the young the promise of a coming maturity which is gentle and peaceful and generous and magnanimous and joyful in its strength.

6

Work and Play

Comparatively little attention has been paid to the subject of work in the history of protestant theology. It is true that the World Council of Churches promoted some studies of the subject under the heading of 'The Responsible Society' after the war and there has been some treatment of it with particular reference to industry in books dealing with industrial mission,[1] but these are recent and not very extensive. The so-called 'Protestant ethic', which is supposed to be an ethic of work, has been much discussed, but it was the discovery of Max Weber, a speculative German sociologist with little direct knowledge of the Anglo-Saxon countries from which he drew most of his material and it has, in fact, received more attention from sociologists, literary critics and publicists celebrating or lamenting its alleged decline than from theologians and church historians. Sermons and popular Protestant literature, especially in Britain and the USA in the late nineteenth and early twentieth centuries, emphasized the virtues of honesty, diligence, punctuality, thrift and self-improvement but this could have been as much a response to the social needs of the time as the result of anything inherent in Protestant theology and ethos. It may be significant that in his book, *The Religious Factor*,[2] which was based on a study of old-established ethnic groups in Detroit, Gerhardt Lenski was able to show that actively practising Catholics exemplified the 'Protestant ethic' almost as clearly as their Protestant counterparts. It was non-practising Catholics who contrived to maintain, even in an American context, the more relaxed attitude to work supposedly characteristic of Catholic culture, especially in peasant societies.

This may be a warning against accepting popular generalizations too readily, even when they come wearing academic dress, but it also underlines how much the matter needs more attention from

43

Protestant theology. This has generally tended to oscillate between uncritical acceptance of assumptions about work current in the milieu in which it is most accustomed to operate, which are those of what is called the 'Protestant ethic' and, on the other hand, a romantic idealism which protests against the inequalities and inhumanities of existing economic orders. So far as it has been influenced by Marxist analysis, it has generally been more preoccupied with its wider social and political implications than with its direct influence on work situations.[3]

This is regrettable because Protestant theology has much to contribute to a Christian understanding of maturity in relation to work. Barth's treatment of the subject, which is itself largely neglected,[4] makes this clear with refreshingly down-to-earth practicality. Work, he says, is necessary for the preservation, safeguarding and fashioning of human life. It has to be carried out objectively, honestly and co-operatively. Stated thus summarily, this may sound abstract rather than down-to-earth, but he specifies in some detail what he means by these, and his treatment has the merit of setting work free from the demonic character which so often belongs to it in the modern world. What Barth is saying, in effect, is that work is there, it has to be done and mankind must get on with it with the minimum of fuss. Yet work must not simply be taken for granted. It is limited by other factors which deserve attention. It is not an automatic but a *human* activity, with self-awareness and appreciation of the struggle involved in overcoming intractable material.[5]

Barth also has practical things to say about the relation between work and vocation. Even when one's work is one's vocation, it is important to distinguish the two, just as it is essential to distinguish the function of the state from that of the church even when the state is composed of committed Christians. Thus, he says, the preacher should take pride in being a good craftsman and his lofty vocation, so far from enabling him to forget this, should lay this obligation upon him all the more firmly. Barth relates how much more satisfactory he found a well-performed variety act he saw one Saturday evening than the bumblingly incompetent sermon he had to sit through on the following Sunday morning, and most of us would readily agree with him. Yet unlike that of a vocation, the work-commitment is a limited one. It is right to ask such questions about any job of work as 'Is it necessary? Could I be more usefully employed?' These are obviously questions which have to be asked with increasing pertinence in the modern world.

This is valuable as far as it goes but, even granting that the professional theologian cannot claim expertise on all aspects of work, is it enough? Work may still reflect the curse of Adam but it can also be creative, and as such it also has to face the problems of success. And this is true not only of vocational work, as in the case of creative artists, but of everyday work also. For example, whatever the precise relation may be between Protestantism and the rise of capitalism, and probably the one thing which can safely be said about it is that any simple account is likely to be misleading, there is manifestly some connection and the fact of this connection is an example of the ambiguity which attaches to success. One hesitates to raise questions over matters where one has no competence, but was Marx doing justice to the situation where he saw the division of labour and the establishment of a distance between the labourer and his work as an example only of alienation? Is it not also a consequence of the employment of scientific method, which abstracts, breaks things down to their component parts and re-arranges them to produce results which yield new meanings and new possibilities? Is not this highly creative, even if it may also sometimes cost more than it is worth because of its de-humanizing effect?

What is undeniable is that it has produced a great deal of new wealth and that, as our argument has led us to expect, this has also created new difficulties. Partly because of the ambiguous way in which the wealth has been created, it has not always been obvious to know what to do with it. Clearly, because the rewards of effort are most unevenly distributed, a great deal of redistribution needs to take place, through taxation and other means, and Christian teaching about mutual dependence should strongly support such moves towards equality.[6] But this is still not enough, because there will be a surplus to spend, and communities will have such a surplus even when individuals do not.

If we are the liberated rich, we badly need a Christian doctrine of how to spend in modern terms. Protestants should be particularly good at this but there is little evidence that they are. Those who believe in justification by faith should have a 'spending' rather than that 'accumulating' ethic which the 'Protestant ethic' is alleged to be, because accumulation leads to work-righteousness, the building up of a treasury of merit. Just as the primary impulse for action in the world for those justified by faith stems from gratitude for what God has done, so the main emphasis of Christians in dealing with the goods and possessions they have, material and spiritual, is on giving, and in doing so with generosity and imagination. So far, little thought has been given to what this should involve. The way taken by most rich protestant individuals and families has been through the establishment of Foundations, where giving becomes a professional exercise. This is a remarkable feature of American life and, when all allowance is made for the tax advantage it may sometimes bring, its beneficiaries should have the magnanimity to acknowledge its generosity and sense of responsibility. Yet, from a Christian point of view, this is only a partial solution because it represents what might be called the clericalism of giving. When offices in the church are over-concentrated in the hands of a professional clergy, it may be a sign of a desire to do things well but it is also an indication of declining vitality on the part of those who are only too happy to hand over functions to the clergy. Similarly, to hand over the disposal of wealth to Foundations is a sign that it is regarded as a serious matter which needs care and attention but also that those who create or inherit the wealth lack the time or the insight to know how to spend it.

In saying this, the last thing I should want to suggest is that we should waste our substance in riotous living, but work creates wealth and wealth, in its turn, creates problems. To know how to spend wealth is at least as much a matter of Christian responsibility as to work hard and to be prepared to make sacrifices. Nor can the problem be solved by giving all our possessions away. It is true that this is what the rich young ruler was told to do, and this is what some may still have to do. It may even be that our whole civilization will not be saved until it learns again what material and spiritual poverty mean.[7] But even to sell all and give to the poor is not a simple operation, and in the complex modern world is could be peculiarly difficult. One has to consider the effect of the disposal of great possessions on their recipients, let alone on the balance of payments. This is even more true of spiritual possessions than of material ones, and it is true enough of the latter. We might be doing no more than wishing our problems on to others, saying to them in effect, 'Here, take them and see whether you can do better,' and we might find the recipients increasingly reluctant to accept them. That has been an element, although in fairness no more than one element, in the attitude with which Britain has divested herself of the colonial responsibilities she has inherited and it is not entirely admirable.

On the basis of what has already been said about the nature of maturity, it is possible to see some of the ways in which the creative power of work should express itself so that it promotes rather than hinders our own entry to the kingdom, and in doing so promotes that of others also.

First, the more successful our work is, and the richer we become as a result, the more important it is to improve the work's quality and to be discriminating about what we do. Most new things have to be bought at a price, and we should become increasingly sensitive to the question of whether the price we have to pay for our prosperity is worth paying, especially when we remember that some of the heaviest bills take a long time to come in. This has become increasingly clear in these days in relation to our material environment when the degree of pollution and ultimate poverty which the pursuit of short-term prosperity involves has become inescapably obvious, but more is involved in it from a Christian point of view than is usually considered. In discussing the church's institutional prosperity, we shall see how vital it is that it should strike deeper roots as it grows if it is not to wither and die in the next generation. This works even more rapidly in the ordinary life of society, especially modern highly industrialized society, because it is always disposed, unless it meets stern resistance, to produce not what is most necessary for the community's health but what can be most readily and profitably made and sold, in the largest possible market, and this means standardization and increasing triviality.

This is why the richer we become, the more we need to educate ourselves for maturity, to be stimulated into new kinds of creative action and to be taught both how to give and how to be more discriminating over what we ourselves consume. Once again, this is as important in relation to the things of the mind and spirit as it is to material goods. Many of the good things of this life are too readily available in these spheres also in the Western world. They are poured out endlessly through modern media of communication, including formal education itself. It has all become more than most of us can take in. The response becomes pitifully superficial because we have not been able properly to 'mark, learn and inwardly digest' one great experience before another crowds in upon us. All this rich diet is proving too much for us, especially as we already show signs of becoming fat and slothful. The only way out, as we have seen, is harder and better work. When we really try to meet our great responsibilities in the modern world, then we shall need and be able to burn up all the energy provided by the good things which are so readily available.

Secondly, work breeds wealth and, in the long term if not always

47

in the short, the better the work the greater the wealth. But wealth stimulates covetousness. The more we have, the more we want. This is partly because it becomes progressively more difficult, and more expensive, to maintain the same level of satisfaction as that which was originally received from the enjoyment of prosperity,[8] and partly because we come more and more to put our trust in our possessions. We both want them to grow and to be secure, to put them out to usury and, at the same time, to place them where neither moth nor rust (inflation) can erode nor thieves (the government) break through and steal. The two aims are incompatible, so we become anxious and deserve our Lord's rebuke. The best cure for this anxiety is better and more useful work, undertaken according to an order of priorities different from that which the pursuit of wealth alone imposes. Experience amply confirms this. When one is absorbed in doing worthwhile work which calls out one's best capacities, anxiety evaporates. Just as great responsibility evokes humility, so worthwhile work demands the concentration which leaves no room for worry. Similarly, no one who finds real satisfaction in his work has more than a marginal interest in the extraneous rewards it brings, such as the size of the pay cheque which is such an endless cause of squalid dispute in these days. He literally has better things to think about. This is true of work in general. It should be supremely true of the work of those who have a vocation to seek first God's kingdom and his righteousness.

This attitude should not only mean release from the curse of covetousness but should also enable us to be generous and joyful. This, in its turn, should affect the way in which wealth is shared and work found and apportioned. Mature Christian civilization should be able to pass on to other societies the benefits, material and spiritual, which wealth has brought it, along with the resources necessary for their proper use, while, at the same time, helping those who receive them learn from its mistakes. The poorer peoples of the world are obviously not well served when they are encouraged to move from the frugal simplicity of a pastoral existence and uproot themselves from their families and the social contact to which they are accustomed, in order to engage in repetitive work in mines or factories and to spend much of their extra money income on baubles which provide dubious satisfactions. The present surge of interest in so-called 'intermediate technology' is a belated recognition of the truth of this. It must not be allowed to have only the short life of a fashionable novelty. It has arisen out of genuine Western self-criticism[9] and its implementation will demand skill and persistence and the readiness to fight powerful vested interests, in the poorer nations themselves just as much as in the richer.

It was the Protestant countries which, for good or for ill, took the initiative in starting the Industrial Revolution. It would be wonderful if they had the will to take a similarly energetic initiative in repairing its damage. They have greater resources for doing so than either they or their critics often suppose. Partly because they are so self-critical, they are often the victims of their own caricatures. The actual ethics of the most characteristically Protestant of Protestant communities in modern times have not borne very much relation to the 'Protestant ethic' of popular sociology. They may have suffered from complacency but they have certainly not been joyless and pinch-penny. More nonsense has been written about the Puritans and their descendants than about any other social group. Even on the material level, it has been countries like Scotland and Holland and Canada and New Zealand and parts of the USA and England which, over the years, have produced many of the finest goods and achieved the highest level of job satisfaction for the largest number of people. One of the greatest, and least regarded, achievements of the USA has been its combination of zest in work with joy in giving, which is very refreshing by comparison with the grumbling shabby-gentility of so much modern British life. This is not due simply to the youth of the nation, as disparaging critics allege, but is an achievement of maturity and, for the sake of mankind, it is to be hoped that recent painful international experiences will only make the USA see more clearly that energy can sometimes be misdirected and that the act of giving needs a long apprenticeship rather than make it throw away this achievement in disgust.

One of the reasons why American work and giving possess these qualities of zest and generosity is that they also have within them an element of play. This is the surest sign that they are the fruit of growing maturity rather than of inexperience. The more we succeed in redeeming work from the curse of Adam, the more like play it should become. 'All work and no play makes Jack a dull boy.' More than that, it is likely to make him a listless and inefficient workman, a worried workman who lacks sufficient detachment and imagination to enjoy what he is doing. Protestants of all people should know this because, if there is anything their basic insights should teach them, it is the dangers of work-righteousness, so that even the most worthwhile, socially useful work, should not be taken all the time with

49

complete seriousness. This is why there should be no Protestant doctrine of work without a Protestant doctrine of play.

Once again, the extent to which traditional Protestant culture has failed to see this point has been grossly exaggerated by its critics.[10] It is not generally known that even John Calvin used to play bowls with John Knox and other friends in Geneva on Sunday evenings and insufficient attention has certainly been paid to the fact that most of the great team games of the modern world were invented and initially developed in Protestant communities.[11] But work-righteousness is so pervasive that it creeps into our play, as any American football coach or British soccer manager can testify, so that even our play needs to be redeemed if it is itself not to share in the curse of Adam.

As far as the inner life of the church is concerned, the place to begin this redemption is with the institution of the Lord's day. The Lord's day is not only the festival of the resurrection but also the day which incorporates, in a Christian context, the insights of the Jewish Sabbath. As Barth has observed, it is appropriate that what was the Sabbath day according to the Genesis story for the creator should be the first of days for his creatures. It is the day on which we are to stand back from our everyday occasions and look at them in the perspective of eternity, taking heart from the knowledge that God's kingdom is our home and rejoicing in the way in which things are moving to the fulfilment of his original intention in creation. The element of play should be present in this sense, that on this day we pretend briefly that we are already redeemed, so that we can return refreshed to face the mundane realities of life on this earth during the rest of the week. The pretence does not lie in supposing that the heavenly country exists when it does not, but in the playful assumption that we are already there while we are still on this earth. This is the real point of reducing all secular activity to a minimum and putting on our best clothes and treating each other with special dignity. The meaning has been lost when this is regarded as an expression of legalism, of 'strictness'. It is meant to be a celebration, a discipline of fulfilment and happiness. We look at each other briefly as though we were already glorified. The Christian vision of the world to come is no impoverished retreat from reality. It is an imaginative apprehension of a life fuller than our present capacities are able to express, so that there has to be an element of pretence, of play, in our attempts to anticipate that life. Yet, as with the play of children, the effort involved in acting the role of being more grown-up than we really are, indirectly trains us for greater maturity and strengthens us for the meeting the more intractable challenges of every day.

The decline of the full enjoyment of the Lord's day, has undoubtedly diminished us, both in our ability to work and to play aright. It is a sign that our horizons have shrunk when instead of looking at our lives in the perspective of eternity, so many people are content to fill up their Sundays simply with journalistic interpretations of the week's events. Christians do sometimes succumb to a false other-worldliness but that is hardly a serious threat at present. The world to come is not only what lies beyond the grave, it is also the world of the future into which Israel believed that their God was calling them and where alone he made known his name as Yahweh, who would reveal his nature only as he called his people into a new situation. This is the basic stimulus to new creation which, in this sense, always has to be other-worldly. It both gives urgency and courage to the effort to bring something new into being and the ability to persevere when the originality of what is being created prevents others from recognizing its value.[12]

The Lord's day will not recover its refreshing quality by being made more relaxing, nor yet, as some liturgical experiments which rightly seek to re-emphasize its elements of celebration try to do, by following the world's fashion of what is supposed to be lively and spontaneous. It has to provide renewal for those who are hungry and thirsty after their struggles in the world and, while it is true that their jaded appetites may need a little judicious stimulation, what they require most is solid sustenance, which builds them up into maturity and gives them strength for the next stages of their journey.

This does not require that the element of play should be overlooked, even in worship. The Lord's day is the minister's main working day, and he should conduct himself with the diligence and competence of a professional, but he should not forget either that he is the leader of a celebration, in the preaching as well as at the Lord's table. Ministers sometimes give the impression on the Lord's day of being more consumed with worldly anxiety than any tycoon determined to keep ahead in the rat-race, rushing to do too many things according to the tightest of schedules, trying like Martha to justify themselves by being cumbered about with much serving. It is on the Lord's day above all else that his people should be those of gentle spirit, peacemakers, magnanimous, generous and joyful. The servants of the church's service can help them become this by keeping the tension and strain involved in their own service firmly in the background and by striving to make public worship express the order and composure, and occasionally the silence, of the world to come.

Their celebration of the Lord's day should be normative for the way in which they enjoy recreation but play has a place on other levels of experience as well, for even the most mature of Christians. It also has a negative justification, as a way of coping with some of the inescapable limitations of our fallen nature. None of us is yet fully redeemed, nor are we likely to be while we remain on this earth. We all suffer from what might be described as the hangover of evolution, possessing deeply rooted within ourselves aggressive and combative and competitive urges, which often make us anything but gentle in spirit and makers of peace and magnanimous, even when we set out with the best intentions of being so. If we pretend that we are entirely free of these urges, we are probably being guilty of humbug, or if they are so weak in us as to be safely ignored then either we are remarkably far advanced on the road to sanctity or, more probably, we are lacking in that natural vitality which is regarded as normally, and even admirably, human. These qualities are very visible in children and we know that controlled play is a civilized way of chanelling and releasing these energies in a harmless, enjoyable and sometimes a socially constructive way. Adults also need games, in which it is right to want to win and to be disappointed if you lose, to be shamelessly and cheerfully partisan and even to show off a little. It is essential, however, that we keep within the rules and that the games be treated as forms of play and not as part of the serious business of living. It is good to play hard but it is essential to play fair and to keep one's sense of proportion. For this reason, Christian maturity has an interest, which our allegedly over-solemn predecessors saw more clearly than we do, in preventing games from becoming too professionalized and linked with politics, national prestige and religion, altogether more serious than work and certainly than vocation. We may again have to enter arenas which used to be centres of recreation but have increasingly become more like places of gladiatorial combat to try to bring back play to sport. Things have reached such a pitch that probably some of us will have to be thrown to the lions in order to do so.[13]

But the positive side of the justification of play is the more important. It may be necessary sometimes to relax from the strains which vocation imposes and behave like children but it should be more characteristic of the followers of Christ to celebrate the strength of their maturity. This is done chiefly through their grateful service of their neighbours, and through the superabundance of that service, but it should also be done through their ability to enjoy themselves and to share enjoyment with each other and to spread enjoyment around. 'See how these Christians love one another,' the surprised ancient world said, and was impressed. The modern world would be even more surprised and impressed if it were compelled to say, 'See how these Christians enjoy one another.' We have become so conscious of strain today that the notion of having a surplus of energy may seem unreal yet mature Christians should occasionally find themselves in situations where they have time and energy to do things for no other reason than to express their joy in living. Only when this kind of mastery is achieved, when, in Augustine's phrase, we use the world to enjoy God and through God are able to enjoy the world, do we come near maturity and can be trusted with success.

7

A Church Come of Age

One of the most tantalizingly elusive sections of Bonhoeffer's *Letters and Papers from Prison*[1] is that in which he speaks of a world come of age and of the difference which this demands in the attitudes of Christian spokesmen. I have taken part in many discussions of what he might have meant, where good arguments have been put forward on behalf of various, and possibly contradictory, interpretations, and have reached the conclusion that, beyond a point, speculation becomes unprofitable. After all, he was not writing a PhD thesis but throwing out a fresh idea in a letter written from prison to a friend. While I am confident, therefore, that the first point I want to make is very much in the spirit of what Bonhoeffer was beginning to express in his *Letters and Papers*, it would be too much to claim his authority for it. The notion of a world come of age demands that we also think of the church as a community of those who have come of age. No Christian believer, least of all one with Bonhoeffer's convictions,[2] can accept the idea that the world reaches any positive maturity without reference to its creator, as though it possessed an independent vitality of its own, which enables human reason progressively to liberate itself into some kind of abstract apprehension of pure truth, uncorrupted by all the errors of the past. This is the possibility which has captivated reflective Europeans ever since Descartes shut himself up in his room beside his stove and resolved to doubt the existence of everything except God and himself as a thinking subject. God gradually dissolved into nonentity as a result of this process and finally Sartre and others discovered that the thinking subject itself also dissolved, leaving only intolerable contingency, with which no one can live. If there is any positive sense in which the world has come of age, it must be because it has been *given* maturity, which means freedom, choice, accountability and limitation, in relationship, in co-humanity. That is to say, it has been given maturity of the same kind as that which is claimed for those who know God in Christ.

The Christian claim is that there is only one kind of maturity, only one form of true humanity, whose nature has been made clear in Jesus Christ.[3] It may have adumbrations and developments in areas of experience which bear no direct relation to the community of Christian experience. What these are and how they are related to Christ is the subject of constant debate within the Christian community itself but the Christian claim loses its point if what is revealed concerning mankind's nature and destiny in Jesus Christ is not normative for the understanding of humanity as a whole. The fact of Christ means that the race has not developed in the way it has by accident but in the providence of God. Christian anthropology stands or falls by the claim that it is true anthropology. This is the theme worked out with such confident amplitude in Barth's *Church Dogmatics* III and IV. The church is intended to be the community which consciously organizes its life on the basis of the belief that, whether it likes it or not, mankind has come of age because, in the fullness of time, God sent his son. This holds for all mankind, but it is the church's responsibility to witness to the universality of this truth by the way in which it expresses the recognition of it within its own life.

If this is so, nothing could be more beside the point than to suppose, as some current Christian discussion seems to, that the world has one kind of maturity and the church another and that the church, therefore, has 'problems' about how to address a world come of age. There may, of course, be circumstances in which those outside the church may be speaking more truly mature words than those within[4] but there are no 'problems' about these which cannot be solved by more genuine obedience on the church's part. In so far as they are words of maturity, they make a bond between those within and outside the church and communication between them becomes that much easier. What the church has to say to the world is essentially the same as what it has to say to itself, although it may find it expedient to use different language in the one case from the other. Our destiny is now clear. Through Christ, we have become the children of God, who have the inescapable burdens and privileges of their freedom. We are grown up. It is time we started to act our age and stopped behaving like infants or adolescents. We must take the sustenance which God provides for adults, meat not milk, and build each other up, so that we can rise to the height of our calling.

This is not only congruous with the spirit of Bonhoeffer, in his insistence that to be Christian is to be fully human and that the church must be in the centre of the village and not at its margin, but it is also in keeping with the basic insights of the Reformation, especially as expressed in Luther's primary tract on the Freedom of the Christian Man. Perhaps it is also worth saying in these days with reference to the doctrine of the church that it is very much in harmony with the authentic spirit of the ecumenical movement, certainly as its leaders at the time of the formation of the World Council of Churches at Amsterdam in 1948 understood it. Their emphasis on the worldwide mission of the whole Christian community and their reaction against narrow clericalism and self-centred denominationalism were an attempt to make the church see that, as the Amsterdam Assembly preparatory papers tried to show,[5] her task is to accept the responsibilities of maturity as humanity come of age.

I hope it will be sufficiently clear by now that this attitude is poles apart from ecclesiastical triumphalism and different also from that Christian neo-colonialism with which the ecumenical movement is sometimes charged. It is true that the church is committed to trying to make life on this earth a colony of heaven and that this must arouse the resistance of those whose loyalties lie elsewhere, but her safeguard against making this merely another form of human arrogance is that her first and chief enemies are those of her own household, not those who claim openly to serve other gods. She cannot offer a share in her maturity to those outside or presume to build on any maturity she already finds in the world until she has begun to act her own age. And this she cannot do until she takes into account all that has been said about the perils of riches.

The dangers of triumphalism, and of Christian imperialism, arising from pride, can never be discounted but more characteristic of churches today are those which come from complacency and sloth. Barth speaks of dispiritedness as an advanced form of the sin of sloth and it is that dispiritedness, together with the mean and shrunken imagination which goes with it, which afflicts Christendom today. This may be more true of Britain than America, especially since the ecumenical movement has lost much of its momentum, but there are wide reaches of American church life also, especially in older parts of the country, where it is not absent.

Any sociologist morbid enough to be interested in ecclesiastical pathology could easily divide churches according to the different ways in which they are guilty of settling contentedly for less than maturity. There are those who treat all, or nearly all, members of the church merely as ordinary human infants rather than those who enjoy the glorious liberty of the sons of God. Either the laity are regarded as the dependent children of the clerical hierarchies who are called 'Fathers' and who alone enjoy varying degrees of adult status, or else clergy and laity alike become merely childish, as happens in some forms of popular Protestantism, with the clergy fulfilling a role not unlike that of permissive primary school or kindergarten teachers. Or else, when a little more vitality is present, the church is regarded as a school of spiritual adolescence, whose members constantly exhort each other to be prophetic, or even revolutionary, and who are at odds with the generation immediately before them, while they eagerly reach out after responsibilities in which they lose interest once they are handed to them, all as ways of resolving their identity crisis.[6] This is a much healthier situation than the others, but a church growing towards maturity will be glad to pass through it as quickly as possible.

The most typical way in which churches deny their maturity is by behaving as though they have already retired. A contemptuous European once described America as a country which has passed from barbarism to decadence without going through the intervening stage of civilization. That is an observation so grotesquely unfair, except perhaps in relation to some aspects of the American communications industry, as to warrant no comment but an indignant snort, but it has to be admitted that a process not unlike that can be observed in the life of some churches, in America and elsewhere. They may have started in a flush of evangelistic zeal but failed to develop an effective spiritual and intellectual tradition or to abound in the works of love. They may have tried to keep going for a time with doses of revivalist shock-treatment but finally settled into stale routine, resisting all change and stirred only by nostalgia for an idealized past. Such churches are to be found mainly in Protestantism but there are others, chiefly Roman Catholic or Orthodox, which seem to be able to maintain themselves in an attitude of more graceful retirement almost indefinitely, especially in climates, like those of Mediterranean lands, which are conducive to longevity if you are careful not to overstrain yourself.

The fact that so many churches have declined in this way means that the Christian community has a great deal still to do before most of its members can speak with any credibility to the world about acting with maturity. We ourselves have to see that the purpose of church order is not to consolidate existing institutions but to build up the people of God into maturity and we have to be fully aware of how complicated an operation this is, which needs all the resources of the Spirit if it is to be achieved. This is the theme of the New Testament document most directly concerned with maturity, the letter to the Ephesians. Having celebrated Christ's victory over all the alien powers which try to make human life subservient to them, the writer prays that his readers may appropriate the rich heritage which is now theirs and know the power of God in whom the fullness of life dwells. The second chapter asks them to remember their former alienation and emphasizes the breaking down of all barriers in Christ, so that they can be built up into Christ in co-humanity. The third chapter carries on the theme of the richness of this inheritance, which is open to Gentiles as to Jews, and prays that they too may comprehend what is the breadth and length and height and know the love of Christ which surpasses human knowledge. The fourth appeals to them to live up to this high calling and moves on to the classic passage in which it is explained how all the gifts of the Spirit, made available through the ascended Christ, are intended to promote their growth into maturity, which they find together in Christ. The rest of the letter is taken up with reminders of some of the ethical consequences of this and concludes with the appeal to put on the whole armour of God.

From the point of view of growth in the common life of the church perhaps the key-word is that of building-up, or edification. Two particular aspects of it need bringing out in this context. The one is the generous nature of the provision made for it and the other is that all these gifts can only be properly appropriated when they are shared. Rich growth on good soil and co-operation in growth, these are the marks of a living church. We have all received an undeserved legacy and as we gather together for the share-out, we discover that the conditions are that we have to use it and multiply it and do this in the only possible way, by co-operating with each other. To take one's own portion and go off to spend it in a far country on one's own is to waste it and to deny the purpose of the whole enterprise.

The way of the world, mercifully tempered by natural affection and our common interest in self-preservation, is not to build each other up but to do each other down. It is precisely when we have a chance to build, and not merely to survive, that most of us are tempted to be egotistical, self-assertive and competitive, envying each other's gifts and seeing them as threats rather than as reinforcements. So to deal with each other that we bring out the best in each other requires grace, which bears with it all those qualities which we have been considering. And it has to be genuine grace. If it is reduced to a technique, a way to win friends and influence people, it becomes exploitative, an indirect way of doing others down, or when it is not that, it is sentimental, covering up the realities of the situation and therefore not enabling us 'to speak the truth', or 'deal truly with one another' as it has been alternatively translated, in love and thus to grow into Christ.[7]

This is why Christian growth must always have maturity clearly in view as its goal. The encouragement, the building up, we give to each other has to be more than that of the nursery or of sub-adolescence. These are appropriate on some levels, for babes in Christ or, perhaps, for those so bruised and battered by the cruelty of the world or the misusings of religion that they need tender handling, but the needs of such people must not be the norm, as some forms of modern religious education and pastoral care make them out to be. If we are to help each other grow up, our attitude to ourselves and to each other must have a certain astringency. Our words to each other are to be with grace, but also seasoned with salt. One of the more unfortunate translations in modern ears of the word *parakletos* in the Fourth Gospel is the 'comforter'. There is indeed legitimate Christian comfort, but it comes after, not before, struggle. It only comes at times when it is comfort rather than stimulus that we really need. The word a 'comforter' used to be used in Britain for the rubber dummy put into a baby's mouth for it to suck, and it was thought to be both unhygienic and to hinder weaning. In the nine-teenth century, the flannel band wrapped around a child's middle to protect it against the winter's blasts was also called a 'comforter'. Many people regard religion as no more than the provision of a comforter in these senses. The better translation of *parakletos*, of course, is the 'fortifier' or 'bracer', the one who pulls us together and makes us face life as it is. There is an old Oxford story of Dr Phelps, a Victorian provost of Oriel College, who maintained the ancient English practice of self-torture, now greatly neglected under decadent American influence, of taking a cold bath every morning, regardless of the weather. One raw winter's morning, an undergraduate passing the open window of an unheated bathroom, overheard a stern voice addressing its owner, 'Be a man Phelps, be a man', followed by a splash and a gasp. That is the kind of spirit in which believers should frequently encourage themselves and each other, if they are to be built up into maturity.

The nature of the church's basic ordinances makes it clear that this is the intention of the distinctive structure which the Christian community is meant to have in the world. Baptism, standing at the very door of that community, should have more of the nature of Dr Phelps' experience than it has come to have in most churches. Without at this stage going into the vexed question of whether baptism should always be by immersion and the related question of whether it is right to baptize infants – and much can be said on both sides of these familiar issues – it cannot be denied that baptism by immersion, especially in cold northern climes, does have the advantage of underlining dramatically the only terms upon which new life in Christ is possible. It involves taking the plunge, a shock to the system, and it is natural that we should tremble on the brink.[8] This element must be retained in the structure of the life of the Christian community if growth into maturity is not to be misconceived as a natural flowering, with no awareness of radical discontinuity. If the baptism of the infant children of believers is to be justified, it can only be on the grounds that this awareness of discontinuity is so important that it must be a factor in the upbringing of the child in the Christian community from the very outset.

The Lord's supper must be understood in the light of the same insight. The grace given in baptism must constantly be renewed if we are to be maintained in our new life. It is a life of struggle and we are in persistent danger of falling away while, as we have seen, our very successes bring their own special temptations. This is why we need to be recalled sharply to the reality of our Lord's death and to the need to continue to show it forth until he comes. This does not diminish the Lord's supper as a eucharistic occasion, as a celebration, but it is necessary as a reminder of the only terms on which we can participate in our Lord's victory without being corrupted by what it brings us. Likewise, its emphasis on the corporate character of our life in Christ is a reminder in the same breath that, as Paul had to tell the Corinthians on the very occasion when he recalled the words of institution, our gathering together may itself become a way of doing each other down rather than of building each other up unless we discern the Lord's body in the midst and forgive each other and establish our relations with each other afresh as members of his body.

It is from this point of view also that the proclamation of the Word must be considered. If more is said about this, it is not because it is necessarily more significant than baptism and the Lord's supper – in these days when Christian spokesmen can so easily say the wrong things, these actions may be more effective forms of proclamation – but because it provides the most readily articulated example, in Protestant churches especially, of the way in which the ordinances of the church are meant to be directed towards building up.

At the outset, it must be made clear that church proclamation is much more than a matter of sermons delivered by professional ministers. The Reformed tradition has undoubtedly suffered because, in practice, it has tended to identify the two.[9] Christ is known only in co-humanity. It is the whole body of the church, therefore, which proclaims Christ. We have to proclaim Christ to each other, in the mutual dependence of the body, where each part counts[10] and to do so together in our relationship with the world. It is a travesty of what is meant to happen to suppose that the Word is delivered to the professional maker of sermons on the Sinai of his study on Saturday mornings, with the telephone off the hook so that no one can interrupt his hot line to the Almighty, and then passed on to the waiting people on Sunday morning, when they take a brief holiday from their customary worship of the Golden Calf. For any minister to imagine such a thing is either to fall into an egotistical complacency which disqualifies him from hearing the Word or else, if he is more aware of what is involved, to try to carry a burden of responsibility greater than any individual can bear, precisely the burden which has been removed from our shoulders by our Lord in his declaration of the Word.

It is Christ who speaks the Word, and he does so in the Spirit through the testimony of prophets and apostles as the scriptures record it and through what his people come to know of him in his dealings with them throughout the ages. For the hearing and the continued proclamation of the Word, his people receive gifts, and these gifts are varied in character. 'Some are gifted to be apostles, some prophets, some evangelists, some pastors and teachers to equip God's people for work in his service, to the building up of the body of Christ.'[11] It is true that, whether rightly or wrongly, the exercise of many of these gifts, although not all of them, has been concentrated in Protestant churches in the conventional action of the delivery of sermons in the course of public worship. These exercises have often, although by no means invariably, proved themselves throughout the ages to be truly edifying. But the fact remains that, in themselves, they are not the primary form of the proclamation of the Word of God in Christ by the church. They are a help, designed to enable the church to hear and obey more effectively what he is saying to the whole community. It is a service, to be hoped always a spiritually-gifted service, of the church's service of God. In the sermon, as elsewhere in worship, minister and people wait together upon their Lord. The minister's privilege and responsibility, great enough for any mortal man, is so to lead his Christian colleagues that together they can hear the Word with the maximum of clarity and the minimum of distortion. All his gifts will be needed for this but he will also be dependent on the gifts of the congregation, not least if he is to be helped to get himself out of the way, so that his action is truly one of service and not secretly one of exploitation. To hark back to the analogy with Sinai, the model in this context for the minister is not Moses but Aaron. Moses is the archetype for the apostolic community as a whole, Aaron of his mouthpiece, the minister.[12]

All this should not be taken simply as yet another plea for fewer sermons or for more experiments with other forms of communication within the church. Such experiments may be desirable, although enthusiasts for them do well to remember that, in a time of confusion like the present, they are extremely difficult and the failure rate is likely to be high. We are on safer ground if we begin, at least, by taking more time and trouble to do better what we have been long trained to do and what people have some experience of knowing how to receive from us. That there should be far more interchange between ministers and people about the interpretation of scripture than usually exists today, with far more corporate Bible study and systematic group theological study, is manifest. That hardly comes under the heading of experiment, since there used to be more of this in the past than there is now. In a church growing towards maturity, there should be an increasing diversity of gifts and a growing competence and freedom in self-expression among the members. Experience shows that this will make more and not less demands on the services of the professional preachers of sermons by raising more pertinent questions in the life of the congregation and a more alert and expectant attitude in trying to listen for the answers. This may or may not mean the production of more sermons than we have today. It will certainly mean better ones.

This is an important matter because, even when the sermon is cut down to its proper size, it remains one of the chief ways in which the members of the church, when they gather together, can encourage each other and build each other up. This, above all, is a place where, echoing Bonhoeffer's phrase, we speak to each other in strength and discover what is 'wisdom among the mature',[13] and we badly need to recover the pulpit's proper function. For all the present talk of the decline of preaching and about the need for other forms of communication, there must be as many sermons delivered in churches today as there were in the Victorian heyday of popular·preaching, even though they are certainly very much shorter. What has happened is that less trouble is taken over their preparation, both minister and congregation are more confused about their true function and sermons have become far less significant events. The result is that the growth of the whole church towards maturity is gravely hampered.

What the preacher has to avoid should be obvious enough. He does not talk down to people, nor does he 'chat them up', a procedure normally associated with attempted seduction. Above all, he does not trivialize the material committed to his charge. If he is to help them hear the Word, he has to do his part in enlarging the understanding and the imagination of his hearers, and this means effort and strain on both sides. He must totally reject what still passes for the sermon in too many congregations, the serving of re-hashed everyday trivia about the surface of events, washed up on polluted metropolitan shores and salvaged by beachcombing journalists. His professional responsibility is to help his people hear and understand the Bible, and with it the best wisdom of the Christian past, and this requires a competence and thoroughness and accountability to his peers at least equal to that with which other members of the great professions discharge their responsibilities. But it must also exemplify the qualities of maturity, together with the most acute sensitivity to its dangers. No one who has tried it will pretend that this is easy. Great efforts of translation and interpretation are necessary before people can be helped to hear the veritable Word of God on levels sufficiently deep to nourish real growth. The trouble with a great deal of modern preaching is that it has concluded that the task is impossible before it has been tried, or tried with a degree of effort remotely commensurate with the magnitude of the task. It has fallen into Barth's sin of 'dispiritedness', an advanced form of the sin of sloth.

Two things within the competence of churches as they exist today are necessary if the pulpit is to recover its proper function in ministering to growth toward maturity. The first is the re-establishment of rigorous professional standards in relation to the theological task, which must be undertaken if sermons worthy of the name are to be produced again. It may be valuable also to learn the arts of successful communication in the modern mode but that is, at best, a supplement to and no kind of substitute for the preacher's distinctive task. It remains as true as it ever was that if we take care of the sense, the sound will, in the end, take care of itself. It is a corruption of the Reformed understanding of the church when the professional ministry is thought of as the source of all the gifts which should inhere in the Christian community – those of counselling, administration, initiative, education, healing, social service, prophetic leadership. All are valuable and some may need so to be structured as to have their own professionalism. It is to be expected that the minister of the Word will possess one or more of these gifts as well as those which belong to his own function but it must not be assumed that he should possess all of them. He is not a spiritual 'leader',[14] which is a dubious secular conception. When the expectation is that he should be, the good Lord tends to confound the church by denying the gifts of ministry to her and leaves her only with a kind of failed leader, the pathetic general dogsbody which too many ministers appear to have become. The minister's specialism is the service of the Word and, if he exercises it diligently, as 'a workman not ashamed', he will again compel attention by the way in which he brings out the quality of the material he has to handle.

This will do more than anything else to help bring about the other condition which must be fulfilled if the pulpit is to function properly again. The other members of the church must regain a right understanding of their own function within the church. When there was a sharp decline in the number of candidates coming forward for ministerial training in the USA several years ago, a church 'organization man' explained it as being due to the renewed emphasis on the vocation of the laity, which was such a feature of the ecumenical movement in the forties and fifties. People were beginning to conclude, he said, that they could be good Christians without having to become professional ministers. If that were really the case, which I do not believe for a moment, the churches of the present time have been saved from having to carry the burden of a large number of bad ministers. Once again, the greatest stimulus a professional minister can obtain for doing his own job properly is to find other Christians doing theirs, and thus developing an appetite for the food he exists to help serve to them.

This is why a church growing into maturity will be careful so to organize itself that other members as well as professional ministers will have opportunity to 'deal truly with each other in love', which will include taking initiatives in relation to interpretation of the Word as well as commenting on interpretations offered by the minister. This is particularly true of those who carry heavy responsibilities in the general life of mankind and who may be given insights denied to the professional minister unless he is prepared seriously to listen to them as their servant. Perhaps the gravest weakness of a clericalist conception of ministerial office is that it prevents this from happening, and thus impoverishes the church's understanding of what God is saying to all his people.[15] I do not much like the phrase 'lay theologians' but a church growing towards maturity will possess many members of that type.[16] It was a sign of genuine revival when, largely under the influence of the ecumenical movement, so many of them emerged in the immediate post-war period, as it is a sign of decline that their numbers now appear to have diminished. Some progress has been made in the meantime in filling up the missing half of the church's life. The pews are not as comfortable, nor their occupants as somnolent, as they were, but the churches are still over-clericalized. The 'godly discipline' of the Reformed tradition, interpreted in the charitable, life-affirming spirit of the New Testament, remains extremely fragmentary even in those churches which are proudest of their Reformed heritage. In these days, they are often put to shame by the way in which the 'apostolate of the laity' is fulfilled in the Roman Catholic Church. Until this situation alters, we shall continue to provide clearer examples of the consequences of complacency and sloth than of what mature humanity can be.

Even in this situation, however, churches are not without their riches, and therefore also the problems which riches bring. In particular, they possess the inheritance of the institutional remnants of past success. A clear understanding of what maturity means can do a great deal to help them deal with these in ways which promote and do not frustrate their true purpose.

To illustrate, a living church usually grows, numerically, financially and as an organization, as well as in terms of spiritual maturity. That is, she inevitably becomes an institution, occupying a 'space' in the world, in Bonhoeffer's phrase, but for many practical purposes it is no different from the spaces occupied by other institutions. She undertakes other functions than the maintenance and the reflection upon the means of grace. She becomes an employer of labour, an educational establishment, a social service organization, a caterer, and much else beside. It is not always appreciated, even by church people, what a great deal of space churches do occupy in the world. The Roman Catholic Church is reputed to be the largest single employer of labour, apart from some state military and civil establishments, in the whole world. This is inevitable, and can be done with grace, but a church has to see that her very success along these lines will interfere with her growth towards maturity unless she has at least these two considerations in mind.

First, she will be at pains to distinguish clearly between her various institutional functions and have very firm priorities. Of all bodies, she should know that the more good things are added unto her, the more her earthly kingdom expands, the easier it becomes to lose sight of the fact that she is meant first to seek God's kingdom and his righteousness. Apart from anything else, if she fails to make these distinctions, she will use on one level attitudes and procedures which are appropriate only on another. That is the road to the sanctimonious incompetence which disfigures some church organizations. Thus, it is right for the church to ask her members to make sacrifices for the sake of the kingdom, 'to give and not to count the cost; to fight and not to heed the wounds; to toil and not to seek for rest; to labour and not to ask for any reward' but, in doing so, she must be quite sure that it is for the sake of the kingdom that she is asking them, and not for some everyday purpose of the church as one earthly organization among others. The relation between the kingdom and the church is never one of identity and it is only the Lord, and never any church official *ex officio*, however personally dedicated he may be, who has the right to ask for that kind of sacrifice because it is only he who can lead us to the level of experience where strength can be found genuinely and acceptably to make it. To use the fact that a call to such sacrifice is always a possibility, and that we must keep in training to be ready for it, as an excuse for tight-fistedness or sharp practice in the ordinary relationships of life is to be guilty of the sin of Simon Magus (Acts 8), generally in these days without being able even to offer the slight compensation of a share in the excitement of his false charisma.

Likewise, as one organization among others in the world, the church should nevertheless behave as a community of the rich, but one which has been made to realize the perils of riches. What is distinctive about her attitude is that she should do this regardless of whether, by the standards of the world around her, she happens to be materially well off or not. To take an example from what is sometimes thought of as one of the most delicate matters of all, that of the payment received by those concerned most directly with the service of the sanctuary, professional ministers. In Britain since the

Second World War – the situation is significantly different in the USA where the churches have enjoyed more recent institutional prosperity – churches have had relatively little money with which to pay ministers and, let it be said, even less with which to pay other servants of the sanctuary like church musicians. In itself, this need not matter very much. Those who perform these services are not in it for the money and, in the things which matter most, they are rich people, but the attitude which a church adopts in such a situation matters a great deal. Suppose a church were to say to a minister, or to any other paid church officer: 'You know the situation as well as we do. We cannot pay you as much as we should like and we know, of course, that it is not comparable to what you could probably obtain doing other work, but it is the best that we can do. As soon as things improve, we shall not need any prompting from you to see that you share fully in our good fortune, and any suggestion you have about making things easier we shall most sympathetically consider. The important thing is that we all do our best to ensure that you are set free as much as possible for your essential task, which cannot be computed in monetary terms.' In a situation like that, most ministers can accept low pay cheerfully and the attitude of their congregation helps to build them up, to make them appreciate how rich they really are.[17] But if a church gets into the frame of mind where it feels self-righteous about the poverty of its paid servants and assumes that it need not be unduly concerned about it because the going rate in this particular market has usually been low, this inevitably breeds resentment which drags down and impoverishes both ministers and people. The trouble lies not in unavoidable material poverty but in a thoughtless misuse of the riches of dedication and loyalty on which the church can call. Like all rich people, churches like to have large numbers of domestic servants and they should be sufficiently gracious, and aware of the temptations of riches, to know how to treat them aright. The church's inner life must express the considerate, harmonious, generous, magnanimous and joyful nature of the gospel by which she claims to live.

The other consideration is no less fundamental. The church exists to proclaim the good news of where true humanity is to be found and to exemplify in the midst of this present world what growth towards maturity in Christ means. This is why the Spirit calls people out of the world and gathers them into church order, which is much more than institutional organization since it is meant to reflect the order of the coming kingdom rather than that of this world which is passing away. For this purpose, they need to assemble frequently to spend much time together, to offer praise and prayer, to encourage and build each other up and to wait upon the Lord in his Word that they may consider re-ordering their lives in the light of his will as they strive to move towards the fullness of their life in Christ. All this most Christians recognize. What is not so widely recognized is that, having gathered, they must also scatter. Their life is not meant to be lived only in the fellowship of believers. That would make them again to be a saved remnant out of the world rather than a saving remnant in the world. They have to move out into the world, both in order to bring others to the knowledge of the truth and to express their vows of obedience in their daily lives, striving to transform the common life of this passing world into the image of the coming kingdom. A church which tries to grow towards maturity will see that its growth depends as much on effective scattering as upon gathering and it will never allow the one to suffer at the expense of the other.

While the professional ministry must inevitably be preoccupied with what happens to the church when it gathers, it has an equal responsibility to help ensure that, having gathered, it also scatters. One of its modest achievements in several Western lands in the years immediately after the Second World War was that some of its members took the initiative in encouraging that revival of Christian vocation in the world which took place at that time, expressed by the many activities promoted by or associated with the World Council of Churches. This did not happen quite as much in the USA as it did in Europe, partly perhaps because the need for it was not so glaringly obvious, and it may be important for American churchmen to bear this in mind in planning their strategy for the future. The last thing I should want to do is to disparage the great church-building boom which the USA experienced in the period up to the early 1960s, which has already suffered from being undervalued rather than otherwise. The opportunity for horizontal expansion was there and it was right to thrust in that particular sickle with all the vigour which the lively American churches possess. The amount of devotion and sheer hard work which went into the enterprise deserves the respectful admiration of the rest of the world's Christian community. Yet the temptation obviously existed to regard ecclesiastical empire-building as equivalent to the extension of the kingdom and thus to create an ever-larger buffer state between the kingdom and the world, having its own laws, customs and internal taxation system. When, as always happens with such booms, the period of expansion ends and the problems of maintaining this over-extended empire in the style to which it has become accustomed multiply, the danger then is that those who have a vested interest in keeping it going, who are chiefly those professionally employed within it, will spend all their energies in dealing with its internal problems and become increasingly reluctant to encourage its members to scatter.

American resilience and self-criticism, along with continuing national expansion, may prove sufficient to enable her churches to avoid some of the mistakes which the British churches committed in the aftermath of their Victorian boom, but only if they see where the dangers lie. In their proper desire for greater unity, and the redeployment of resources which it ought to bring, church administrators should seek to prevent the creation of excessively large and complex new church structures, which take too many people and too much time and money to maintain and which, therefore, inevitably increase the size of the ecclesiastical buffer-state at the very time when it should be contracting. On the other hand, the line taken by some 'activist' young ministers in Britain and America in recent years is no less misleading. This is that they themselves should do the scattering and devote most of their energies to social work, general education or political activity, calling these good works expressions of their distinctive ministerial functions. This is a misuse of their calling and implies a covert clericalism which would be as damaging to the integrity, and maturity, of the church as the overt clericalism of earlier times, if it had any hope of being anything like as effective. The professional minister can best serve the church's service in the world by so interpreting the faith for people in church that they are eager to clear off church premises to get on with their real job, once the worship and the study and the discussion and enjoyment of each other's company and the care for each other which should follow it are over. The presence of church mice finding room to make their nests on church premises is a sign of bad housekeeping. One very practical way in which ministers can help them clear off is by keeping church councils and committees and their agendas to the barest minimum and by setting an example to such activities in the outside world by the economy and dispatch with which the church's internal business is dealt with. Quaker meetings may not be a fully adequate form of public worship but other churches can learn things from them about the way in which their business should be conducted, not least the value of silence when nothing significant requires to be said and the promptness with which the meeting closes once the hour is struck. A mature Christian community should not need to spend much time in dealing with the details of its domestic affairs. These easily become a form of that 'anxiety' rebuked in the Sermon on the Mount. There is much more urgent work to be done out there in the world. But it is to be done by those who have the responsibility and calling to do it, and it is officious for professional ministers to try to take that work from them, while still wishing to be regarded as professional ministers.

This is not to say, of course, that ministers of the Word should not stand alongside their fellow-Christians in the world, and do so outside church premises. In the complexity of modern life, the need for chaplaincy constantly grows. It is true also, as it always has been, that when there is an urgent need in the world which no one else can meet, the minister has as much responsibility as anyone else for meeting it. Bonhoeffer found himself driven to such a situation and it could be argued that things might not have come to such a pass in Germany if many other Lutheran ministers had come to the same conclusion much earlier. But that is not the same as saying that such activity is a form of the specialized ministry of the Word. This was something which had to be done and there was no one else to do it. Any Christian might find himself in such a situation and to assume that it is a form of the ministry of the Word because a professional minister knows no exemption from it is dangerously to confuse functions. It also sometimes leads ministers to claim privileges which are justified only for the fulfilment of their proper office in contexts where they have no right to them. Clerics who enter the political arena, for example, sometimes claim protection from 'the heat of the kitchen' because they wear clerical collars and should be spared the kind of personal criticism from opponents which ordinary politicians have to learn to put up with.

Maturity is concerned with freedom, choice, limitation, responsibility and accountability. This means that it is the person in a particular situation, whether in church or in private life or in the general life of society, who is answerable to God for the way in which he or she behaves. The minister is there to help and the closer he can get to that person in doing so, without getting in the way, the better. What the minister of the Word cannot presume to do is to take the decision for him or to usurp his place. Ministers who truly understand what their function is in trying to promote growth towards Christian maturity will be more than content with their distinctive ministerial role. It will take all their time and talents to be reasonably competent Aarons without aspiring to be Moses as well.

8

The Inter-Relation of Church and Society

A church growing towards maturity will also strive to have a mature attitude to the wider society in which it has its own space. The way to begin doing so is by considering the church as an institution in the context of other institutions of society with which it is bound to be involved. That may seem obvious enough but the fact is curiously neglected in most discussions of the relation between churches and society. A great deal of attention has been paid, of course, to what the attitude of churches should be to other institutions, and of what the attitude of these others should be to churches, but it has generally been with a view to safeguarding the institutional freedom, and sometimes the privileges, of churches, or else to ensuring that their interests are adequately reflected in the arrangements made by other bodies over matters where churches conceive themselves to be very directly concerned, such as the education of children or laws dealing with family life and sexual morality. And there is a vast body of material produced from a Christian viewpoint about the state, the economic order, education, international affairs, race relations and a whole range of matters of public discussion. Yet, in all this, it has not been common for theologians, in particular, to see the church as one institution, or group of institutions, among others in the general life of the world, itself an important factor in the give and take of social relationships.[1]

One reason for this may be that many of the theologians most deeply concerned for the well-being of society have had more radical views about society than those most deeply concerned for the institutional well-being of the church. This has been especially true of those elaborately structured and centralized churches, like the

Roman Catholic, which would be most likely to be involved as major institutions with other institutions. They have felt embarrassed, therefore, about bringing the church as an institution into the discussion because its own practice often appears to contradict what they are advocating for society as a whole. It has only been quite recently, over a few quite specific issues such as investment policy as it affects race relations, and the status of women, that there has been a partial change of attitude. It was noteworthy that Reinhold Niebuhr rarely applied the insights of his *Moral Man and Immoral Society*[2] to the institutional life of churches even though, on the face of it, they had as much relevance there as anywhere else, and would have given ample scope for the play of his highly developed sense of irony. This may be partly explicable in American terms because the USA does not have that organic view of the whole of society, including church life, which is particularly characteristic of the more traditionalist forms of English society and prefers, as the Constitution lays down, to emphasize the independence rather than the interdependence of society's major institutions, but this is not the only reason because this gap in thinking also exists in British, and in more general ecumenical, discussion also.

Why should it matter that churches should be thought about in this way? Because it is a sign that they are approaching their task in the world with the concreteness which the New Testament requires. In his analysis of the Pauline notion of the church as the body of Christ, Ernst Käsemann[3] has brought out how very specifically, almost literally, this metaphor was meant. If we take the much-abused term 'secularization', as I prefer to do, in a neutral, descriptive sense to mean the church's attempt to express in terms of the conditions of life in this present world insights which derive from a reality which comes from beyond this world, we can regard the church itself, in the process of institutionalizing itself, as the primary form of the secularization of the gospel. It is the body-ing forth of Christ's Spirit in the world. This is bound to have two sides. On the one hand, it represents the victory of faith which overcomes the world. It is an attempt to re-fashion life in this present world which, left to itself, becomes increasingly self-contradictory and destructive, after the form of that which is to come. On the other hand, to the extent to which it succeeds in doing this, the body which it has in the world grows in size and becomes exposed to all the corrupting influences which are abroad in the world. All those forces which are not controlled by the spirit of Christ are able to get to work on it and the more successful the secularization has been, and successful, let it again be emphasized, according to its own criteria of success, the larger and more tempting the target it provides.

What Christian maturity demands of us is the recognition that this process is inevitable, so that we refuse to be surprised or indignant when it takes place and that we call upon the resources which we have for not succumbing to the dangers of success. A restated doctrine of development of church institutional life, as well as doctrine, is badly needed, one which is based on close observation and which is emancipated from Newman's aesthetic intoxication with the idea, rather than the reality, of Catholicism, and one which also does full justice to the inescapably ambivalent nature of the process of secularization, even in the most favourable circumstances within the context of a civilization calling itself Christendom. This has quite astringently practical consequences. If, for example, in all the time it was discussing 'secularization' in general terms, the World Council of Churches had seen this and had looked at itself as one earthly organization among others, in many respects similar to other international agencies which surrounded it in Geneva, it might have prevented itself from moving quite so rapidly in the same direction as many of them, in becoming increasingly elaborate, expensive, bureaucratic and vulnerable to exploitation by organized pressure groups.[4]

There are two rules about the way in which the Christian community should develop as one institution among others in the life of the world if it is to avoid going the way of the world, which are already sufficiently clear to have application today. The first is very simple, but failure to see it still gives rise to misplaced concern. Christian growth towards maturity is best judged in qualitative rather than in quantitative terms. It is not the size of the plant but its health, appearance, taste and power of propagation which matter. This is not to say that, therefore, statistics of membership and of giving are unimportant. Over the long term, if not in the short run, the probability is that a church expanding in these ways is likely to be healthier on more fundamental levels also than one which is steadily shrinking. Yet if the plant is to continue to flourish in the difficult climate of the world, it needs deep roots. The striking of these roots takes time and is not readily visible, and for healthy growth it is more important to nourish the roots than to be efficient in gathering all the fruits. A church which does not strike deeper as her institutional body grows is likely to produce inferior fruit in the next generation and ultimately to wither and die. There is little consolation in seeing

73

the truth of this confirmed in the experience of so many of the churches of popular Protestantism in our own time.

The chief question a church growing towards maturity must be asking itself is not whether it is growing rapidly enough – it could be bolting like a lettuce – but whether its growth is healthy. And this will mean feeding the soil, watering, the ceaseless removal of weeds and occasional pruning and grafting. It also needs a quality of whose importance no good gardener needs to be reminded: patience. Roman Catholicism has shown this quality in its mission to Western lands in recent generations, but it is one which most forms of Protestantism conspicuously lack. Anyone who compares the position of the Roman church in modern England with what it was a hundred years ago, and the same is partly true in the different circumstances of the USA, will see that such patience is sometimes rewarded even in this life. It is true that occasional *kairoi* do come in the life of institutions as well as of individuals, decisive moments when situations have gathered to a head and when it is essential to move in fast with all that one has to make the most of the opportunity, but Christian growth has usually to start from small beginnings. This is particularly difficult to remember when re-planting has to be done on heavily worked soil which has borne good crops in the past. When a plant has grown old, healthy flowers and fruit cannot be maintained without the sowing of fresh seed and going through the long process of maturation. The ground has to be prepared again, and some may have to lie fallow for a time, before vigorous growth can be expected.

Without driving the horticultural metaphor too hard, if there is any truth in this kind of analysis it obviously has severely practical implications for church strategy in a country like Britain today, implications which may have relevance for those metropolitan and run-down rural areas of the USA where the churches also languish. One of the troubles with British church life today is that, in the earlier part of this century when previously prosperous churches were beginning to decline, great efforts were made to revive them by church extension and 'Forward Movement' schemes. Not enough attention was paid to the replenishment of the ground and to replanting in places where crops had already been gathered. The result is that large areas of British society are left, in church life, either entirely barren or inhabited only by scrub and stunted second growths.

The second rule is related to the first, and is equally simple, although it seems to be equally hard to accept. Because churches must expect

74

to share, on the institutional level, in the same cycle of growth and decay which other institutions experience and organize themselves to meet it without thinking that they are failing when they do so, they will strive always to make realistic appraisals of the points in the cycle at which the various parts of their life are likely to be, and conduct themselves accordingly. Again generalizing broadly, churches in most parts of Britain have to face the problems of institutional late middle-age – unlike some other European churches, they do not yet have to face those of senescence. In most parts of the USA – although there are plenty of exceptions, as old-line churches in New England and parts of the South can testify – their problems are those of institutional adolescence. It needs hardly to be said that for institutions to be at an adolescent stage does not carry with it the corollary that the faith of those who belong to them is at the same stage. On the contrary, it is a proof of maturity when members of churches can recognize this about their institutional form, so that they know what problems and opportunities are likely to arise and draw on the experience of the Christian past in meeting them. What matters is that we do our part to help it 'act its age' in God's sight, whether it means moving to the fulfilment or to the restoration of maturity. Only thus can churches overcome the natural tendency of all institutions to reach a peak and then decline, and only thus can they find renewal, even when they are old.

Churches need to remember these things about themselves as they look at themselves as institutions in the setting of the general life of society, but they need also to remember that, as they move out into a wider world, they should become progressively less interested in their own institutional well-being and more and more in that of the world which they claim to serve. This gives a measure of justification to the relative indifference of someone like Reinhold Niebuhr to the relevance of his ideas to the institutional life of churches. From the point of view of his own calling, he could plead that he had more urgent matters to think about. A church is at its most mature when it is forgetting itself in helping the other parts of the life of the community reach their own maturity, as that in its turn is to be understood in a Christian context. This it cannot do unless it gladly recognizes their own autonomy. The other institutions of society are not answerable in the first instance to the church but to God. From this point of view, the American notion of a free church in a free state can be seen as a mature acknowledgment of the need of each for independence from the other if the maturity of each is to be fulfilled although, to British eyes, the height of the wall of separation built by the Constitution may also prevent sufficient interplay between them.

It is true, however, that experience shows that this relation between churches and the other institutions of society is likely to be most effective when the influence of the one upon the other is indirect. Why this should be so I have tried to work out, with particular reference to the example of educational institutions, in my book, *Beyond Religion*.[5] It is a sign of vitality when a church gives birth to another institution, as it has to many in the course of history, and it can do a great deal to nourish and protect it in its infancy, but it represents success, not failure, when that institution wants to be independent, and to stand on its own feet. A mature church will be thankful that this child is now off its hands and will look around for other useful work to do in the world.[6]

A church which understands what coming of age means will know that it will be weakened and vulnerable itself as long as the other significant institutions of the society in which it is set, and in which many of its own members have to carry responsibility, are immature or in decline. The difficulties confronting churches in modern Britain are not unconnected with a more general weakening of community life and the difficulties in which educational establishments and political parties and industrial firms and families and even sporting organizations, find themselves. They will not be solved by the one in isolation from the others. In a time when they have their own full share of such difficulties, churches will testify most clearly to the fact that they are on the way to maturity by the way in which they cease to be anxious for their own life and help their members as they play their part in helping the other institutions of society to which they belong to act their own age as those who are responsible in their own place to their creator.

Notes

1. SCM Press, 2nd ed 1971, pp. 56–9. All following references are to this edition.

2. 'Since the issue of events then, success, is in the hands not of men but of God, the pilot of history, it is not a cowardly opportunism, but the truly fruitful relation to history, when we, whether as victors or vanquished, turn our attention to historical success and attribute ethical relevance to it' (*Reality and Faith*, Vol. 1, Lutterworth Press 1971, p. 301). What that ethical relevance might be we are not told.

3. G. C. Berkouwer, *The Triumph of Grace in the Theology of Karl Barth*, Paternoster Press 1956.

4. There are a few pages about success near the end of *Church Dogmatics* IV.3.ii, pp. 747–51 (T. & T. Clark 1962), but they are chiefly concerned with the church's lack of worldly success and with the attitude it should show in the face of this apparent failure.

5. This is not to deny, of course, that the gospel is good news, first of all, to the poor and that it cannot be properly received until we are aware of how impoverished we are without it. But once we receive Christ, we are rich.

6. Eph. 4.13 (RSV).

7. Notably in *Church Dogmatics* III.1, pp. 288–9.

8. Eph. 4.14 (NEB). It is ironical that Nietzsche should have come to regard Christian spokesmen as, in effect, such rogues and schemers, producing a morality for slaves which justifies failure.

9. See the discussion of 'The Concrete Place' in Bonhoeffer, *Ethics*, pp. 66ff.

10. Mark 7.27–9.

11. I have tried to work out some of its implications for the Christian community in my own country in my book *The British: Their Identity and Their Religion* (SCM Press 1975). If I resist the temptation to discuss this theme with reference to the 'liberation theology' propounded by South American and other so-called 'Third World' theologians, it is not because I do not recognize its importance, or the fact that it has implications for Christian responsibility in my own situation, but because my own identification with the situations out of which it has arisen is, as yet, so inadequate that any comments I might have to make about it are unlikely to have much pertinence.

12. This is a point brought out well in Robert M. Brown's *New Frontiers for the Church Today*, OUP, NY 1974.

13. It is moving to see how this sometimes works even with such natural egotists as professional politicians. Presidents Truman and Johnson are two

such who appear to have been awed into humility by the burdens of their great office, with self-justification re-asserting its familiar sway only after they had served their terms and begun to write their memoirs.

14. Phil. 2.6.

15. 'It is arguably not the Attilas who ride through blood to a throne and maintain their rule by merciless oppression, who achieve the deepest and most perilous domination over their fellows. "What shall it profit a man if he gain the whole world and lose his own soul?" The man who should strain his ears to catch that most searching question is not the man who has enlarged his resources by enterprises as savagely concluded as they were ruthlessly conceived and executed. Rather it is the man whom his fellows with good reason acclaim as their benefactor, who indeed has, almost unknown to himself, enlarged his private image both of himself and his role by singularly generous service to others.' D. M. Mackinnon, *The Problem of Metaphysics*, CUP 1974, p. 140.

Chapter 2

1. He criticizes Bach's St Matthew Passion for failing to bring this out sufficiently (*Church Dogmatics* IV.2, pp. 252f.). In this he may not be entirely fair, because the note of victory is more pronounced in St Luke than in St Matthew, but it is a reasonable comment on the sentimentally pietist libretto Bach used for his choruses, chorales and arias.

2. Jacques Ellul, *Violence*, SCM Press 1969.

3. Matt. 5.10–12.

4. Phil. 4.4–7.

5. In his book *Enough is Enough* (SCM Press 1975, pp. 45–6), John Taylor claims that *epieikēs* derives from the same root as ikon, a likeness, and that it also has the sense of a matching, a toning in with the whole, relating to the way in which all things fit together, cohere, in Christ.

6. See in particular, *The Children of Light and the Children of Darkness*, Scribners, NY 1944.

It is its failure to see this which is the weakness of the fashionable so-called 'political theology' of the present time. It is disturbing to see this failure reflected even in the writing of so perceptive a theologian as Jürgen Moltmann, as expressed in his recent book *The Crucified God* (SCM Press 1973). We can welcome his insistence that faith means liberation and that liberation means identification with the oppressed and their struggle to ach-ieve independence and responsibility. That is a note which Christians need to strike clearly in some parts of the world today. But Christian faith not only makes clear that liberation, if it is genuine, must have social and political implications, for those who are not professing Christians as well as for those who are. It also has a good deal to say about the way in which those implications are to be followed out. In particular, it has very pertinent things to say about the way in which the liberated conduct themselves after their social and political struggles have succeeded and they themselves enjoy power. What is surprising about the last chapter of Moltmann's book is his

78

apparent failure to recognize that it is precisely at that point that the crucified one speaks his most searching and authoritative word to the liberated. It might have been expected that a German theologian, with the experience of the last sixty years in Europe behind him, would need no reminder that revolution which does not clear the ground for reconciliation, which means self-criticism by the victorious and respect for defeated minorities, has little that is Christian about it.

7. This is not the place to enquire into all that the apostle meant by his expectation that the Lord was near. What can be said is that it did not mean indifference to what happens here and now, but a sharpened awareness of moral realities.

8. *Church Dogmatics* III.2, p. 47.

9. Luke 1.52.

10. II Cor. 14.16–18.

11. Rom. 5.3–5.

12. This is something which was always clearly recognized in the classical English educational tradition. See also Bonhoeffer on 'The Natural Rights of the Life of the Mind', and in particular the sketch of the unfinished section on page 159 of *Ethics*.

Chapter 3

1. Dean Kelly, in his interesting book, *Why Conservative Churches are Growing* (Harper & Row, NY 1972, p. 55), quotes what he calls Wesley's Law: 'Wherever riches have increased, the essence of religion has increased in the same proportion. Therefore, I do not see how it is possible, in the nature of things, for any revival of religion to continue long. For religion must necessarily produce industry and frugality and these cannot but produce riches. But as riches increase so will pride, anger and love of the world in all its branches.'

2. The tercentenary of the death of John Milton was celebrated in London in the autumn of 1974. Nothing is more unbecoming than to pass superficial moral judgments on the great figures of the past. Our first debt to Milton is one of gratitude for his mighty achievements and any query concerning possible failings must be qualified by a recognition of the difficulties he had to face – the frustration caused by his blindness, the intensification by circumstances of the isolation which all creative artists need and his disappointment at the failure of the good old cause of the English Revolution, in which he passionately believed. Yet he does appear to have been partly infected by the spiritual pride he so vividly described in Satan, a pride which, for example, made him lose sympathy even before the Restoration with the struggles of Cromwell as he was faced with the practical necessities of government. It has been said that Milton was an independent churchman in a church of one member, but that is no church at all because one is not an ecclesiastical quorum.

3. OUP 1939.

4. To say this is not to imply any disparagement of the non-slothful

elements in the religion and culture of the South and East, from whose traditions the Protestant North may have a great deal to learn.

Chapter 4

1. See especially his *The Point of View of my Work as an Author*, OUP 1939.

2. In *Church Dogmatics*, in various parts of the vast Vol. III, expecially III.1, ch. 45 of III.2, and III.4.

3. Barth reminds us, as many others have before him, that Don Juan is not the hero but the weakling, the hopelessly immature person, in the matter of love.

4. Bonhoeffer, following the Lutheran tradition, does the same when he speaks of marriage as one of what he calls the four mandates (*Ethics*, pp. 179–84). He was denied the opportunity of saying much about it but what hints he gives suggest a surprisingly conservative attitude.

5. After all, there are many aspects of that same past, such as the way in which patriarchs and kings in Israel took polygamy for granted, which few Christians today would think it right to emulate.

6. I John 3.2 (RSV).

7. Eph. 4.4–6.

8. *Church Dogmatics* III.4, p. 167.

9. III.2, p. 287.

10. It is appropriate to refer again at this point to the remarkable section in the *Dogmatics* III.1, pp. 288–329, and also to his highly contentious claim, based on his exegesis of Pauline teaching, that this order of precedence still has its place in the Christian dispensation (*Dogmatics* III.2, pp. 301–16 and III.4, pp. 172–6).

11. See Barth, III.4, pp.176–81, on masculine 'strength' and feminine 'maturity'. What he says may describe a continuing factor in relations between men and women but, on his own showing, should there not be a kind of mutual influence of their characteristic attributes at their best, as men and women grow in grace?

Chapter 5

1. 'The adolescent as a distinct species is the creation of modern social attitudes and institutions. A creature neither child nor adult, he is a comparatively recent socio-psychological invention, scarcely two centuries old. Distinctive social institutions have been fashioned to accommodate him; in psychology he has been made more or less to fit them, moulded by appropriate rewards and penalties' (Frank Musgrove, *Youth and the Social Order*, Routledge & Kegan Paul 1964, p. 13).

2. Expressed even more tendentiously in Professor Musgrove's more recent book on a similar theme, *Patterns of Power and Authority in English Education*, Routledge & Kegan Paul 1971.

3. CUP 1972.

4. See Matt. 11.30.

5. Perhaps professors should cease to head their departments not later

than the age of sixty, taking instead a more functional and less merely honorific emeritus status. And if the Reformed churches are ever to surrender to the Episcopalian demand that they 'take episcopacy into their system', it would only be tolerable from their point of view if bishops ceased to be the font and focus of church order but became instead dignified semi-retired ministers, available for counsel and for taking part in representative occasions but with little executive power and a firm understanding that, in the ordinary way, no new leadership is to be expected from them.

Chapter 6

1. See in particular Horst Symanowski, *The Christian Witness in an Industrial Society*, Collins 1966.

2. Doubleday, NY 1961.

3. See Alexander Miller, *Christian Vocation in the Contemporary World*, SCM Press 1947. The same is broadly true of Catholic theology influenced by Marxism. A different approach was made by the Anglo-Catholic Christendom group, who were influential in England a generation ago, of whom T. S. Eliot was a prominent member. See V. A. Demant, 'Vocation in Work' in *Theology of Society*, Faber 1946, pp. 175–84 and M. B. Reckitt, 'Work in the Crisis of our Culture' in *Our Culture* ed. V. A. Demant, SPCK 1947, pp. 70–96.

4. In *Church Dogmatics* III.4.iii, 'The Active Life', pp. 470–564.

5. This reminds me of an observation in one of Van Gogh's letters, when he explains that his drawing of a loom is different from a straightforward design print because he has to convey the sense of the struggle of the hand involved in using the loom.

6. This is discussed at greater length in the chapter on 'Incomes and Standards of Living' in my *Equality and Excellence*, SCM Press 1961.

7. We have to remember that the rich young ruler was the representative of Israel, which had allowed the possessions she enjoyed as the fruit of faith, her law and the common life she enjoyed in obedience to the law, to become a barrier in the way of the fulfilment of her vocation.

8. It was the economist Pigou who pointed out many years ago the self-defeating character of the pursuit of luxury. The satisfaction derived from lesser luxuries diminishes as greater ones become possible. At one stage, to have any car seems to be the height of luxury, but who is content with a Volkswagen when he might possibly own a Rolls Royce?

9. See E. F. Schumacher, *Small is Beautiful*, Abacus Books 1974.

10. It was a Protestant romantic who conspicuously failed to understand the Reformation, Thomas Carlyle, who preached the doctrine, *laborare est orare*.

11. It is hard to accept comparisons between the allegedly joyless character of play in modern Protestant lands devoted to football, baseball and cricket, in contrast to that in Latin countries whose chief contribution to sport is the bull-fight.

12. This partly explains why so many great creators, especially artists,

have rarely achieved widespread recognition in their own life-times. It is only nowadays, with improved medicine, that some of them are able to live on for long enough after their main creative periods are over to begin to collect some of the rewards.

In reading Welsh history recently I was struck by the way in which, at the time when, in the first half of the nineteenth century, the modern Welsh nation was being formed and the materially poor Welsh countryside was bursting with fresh cultural and political vitality, which matured in later generations and sometimes on distant soil, their great hymns were full of longing for the world to come and their Sundays were savoured as prefigurements of eternity. See *Welsh Rural Communities* ed. Elwyn Davies and Alwyn D. Rees, University of Wales Press 1960, pp. 198–9.

13. Some highly successful, and no less highly rewarded, professionals in sport make an open confession of their piety and say that it helps their performance. Their witness would be more impressive if it led them sometimes to take light-hearted, and expensive, risks, just for fun, to underline the fact that all this is only a form of play. Professionalism is the clericalism of sport, and needs to safeguard itself against the moral ambiguities of all clericalism.

Chapter 7

1. Dietrich Bonhoeffer, *Letters and Papers from Prison*, The Enlarged Edition, SCM Press 1971, pp. 326ff.

2. See in particular the chapter on 'Christ, Reality and Good' (subtitled 'Christ, the Church and the World') in *Ethics*, pp. 161–84. What one wonders, in the light of his later observations in *Letters and Papers*, is whether he would still have been content with the highly conservative Lutheran interpretation he gives of the 'mandates' in the last part of that section as he considered further the implications of his unitive concept of reality.

3. This of course, will be hotly contested by modern pluralism, some of whose more radical exponents would doubt whether it even makes much sense to speak at all of anything as definite as human nature, while others, with a more positive point of view, argue that it rules out the possibility of learning valuable things about human nature from other religions and philosophies than the Christian one. If this possibility were ruled out, then clearly the Christian claim would need to be restated in such a way as to bring it back in again, because all human experience must be relevant in some way to the understanding of maturity and the claim it makes for itself must be treated with full seriousness. And it is more essential than ever in these days that Christians should realize that our true nature is only in process of being revealed as we move to meet the coming Christ, bearing all in human experience that can endure his scrutiny with us. It is not something simply given to the church, and given to the church as one historical community among others. Once again, it 'doth not yet appear what we shall be'. What we do know is that 'when he shall appear, we shall be like him; for we shall see him as he is' (I John 3.2).

4. See the distinction made by Bonhoeffer between 'hopeless godlessness' within the church and 'promising godlessness' outside it (*Ethics*, p. 83).

5. *Man's Disorder and God's Design* ed. John C. Bennett, SCM Press 1947.

6. One of the troubles with the Western world today is that a great deal of this adolescent vitality has been channelled into vastly expanded academic institutions. This has now excessively prolonged the period of adolescence, denying real responsibility to people who are more than ready for it and need its discipline, while churches and other institutions which could do with this vitality are prevented from receiving it.

7. Eph. 4.15.

8. This is vividly conveyed by Masaccio's 'Baptism of the Neophytes' in the Carmine church in Florence.

9. The Lutheran tradition has, perhaps, suffered even more. It is disconcerting to find Bonhoeffer, even as late as the *Ethics*, stating a sharply clericalist position on this matter, with only a faint gesture in the direction of the necessary distinction and qualifications. 'The book of homilies and the prayer-book are the principal books for the congregation; the Holy Scripture is the book for the preacher; there can be little doubt that this formulation correctly represents the divinely ordained relationship between the congregation and the office' (p. 261). Can there not indeed? Even so relatively conservative a Roman Catholic theologian as Karl Rahner would cast doubt on it in these days. See his *Theology of Pastoral Action*, Burns & Oates 1968, pp. 60–63.

10. Paul makes this point precisely in his discussion of gifts and offices in I Cor. 12.

11. Eph. 4.11–12.

12. And the sensible minister will take due note of the fact that Aaron, with his 'gift of the gab', was a sufficiently insecure and dubious character. No doubt because he was uncertain of his 'role' and sought reassurance of his own 'relevance', it was he who decided, while Moses was tiresomely absent communing with God on Sinai, that there was no alternative but to meet 'the expressed needs of his people' and to supervise the organization of the worship of the Golden Calf.

13. I Cor. 2.6.

14. It is a defect in Hans Küng's otherwise admirable book *Why Priests?* (Collins Fontana 1972) that he still seems to see the ministry primarily in terms of 'leadership'.

15. In view of this, one wonders whether Bonhoeffer would have wanted to continue to defend the conception of the relation between minister and people already quoted from the *Ethics*, especially in the light of his further reflections on the world come of age and speaking to man in his strength.

16. A lay theologian, says one of them, must

1. Be able to read the Bible intelligently.

2. Have a general understanding of what Christian doctrine is and why he believes it on the level of an educated and scholarly adult.

3. Have a knowledge of what is really going on in the world and of what Christian responsibility in public affairs involves.

4. Have devoted thought to the Christian implications and demands of

their own profession, including facing honestly whether it has a right to exist at all.

(W. H. Moberly, *The Crisis in the University*, SCM Press 1948, pp. 269–70.)

This sees things too much in terms of the professional man or public servant – there could be other lay theologians whose vocation lay in very different directions – but it is on the right lines.

17. Most of the creative work of the world has been in the form of unpaid service. This is no argument for not paying ministers, as Paul, himself an unpaid minister, acknowledged, but it is a reason for showing a certain detachment over the whole matter of payment, together with great sensitivity concerning the terms of the relationship where payment is involved.

Chapter 8

1. The essays by Wolf-Dieter Marsch, Frederick A. Shippey and Walter G. Muelder in *Institutionalism and Church Unity* ed. Nils Ehrenstrom and Walter G. Muelder, SCM Press 1963, are refreshing exceptions.

2. SCM Press 1963.

3. Ernst Käsemann, *Perspectives on Paul*, SCM Press 1971.

4. Such a doctrine of development might also be of help to the theology of 'development' in another sense, which is being rightly much discussed in World Council circles today, that of the assumptions on which, and the way in which, so-called programmes of 'development' in relation to those countries which are supposed to need it, are proceeding.

5. SCM Press 1962.

6. This does not mean, however, that she should wash her hands of such children. A continuing relationship which is careful to respect the independence which is a corollary of the maturity of each, may be necessary to the health of both. Once again, however, their very success can create barriers. American theological education provides an example of this. In the past relations between churches and colleges and universities were often creative, even if sometimes in tension, because they had a close relation to each other. The values of the church community had influence upon those of the university and the pulpit was often so imbued with university ideals that it became a significant centre for university extension. Its role in awakening an ambition to give higher education to their children among non-academic people, without which America's phenomenal academic expansion would never have got off the ground, is still inadequately appreciated. But the successful growth of both churches and universities has meant a great increase in the size of both. The result is that it becomes more and more difficult for people, even in theological schools, to have feet in both camps. Each is so big and all-absorbing as to demand full-time, and generally life-long, service and lack of contact increases mutual suspicion and fear, while both suffer from the lack of candid friends who are detached from their day-to-day affairs but on whose judgment, and loyalty, they can rely. It is not surprising, therefore, that their recent success is already beginning to produce evidence of new pride, complacency and sloth in some parts of each set of institutions.